MoviePlus X5
Director's Guide

How to contact us

Web:

Serif Website:	http://www.serif.com
Forums:	http://www.serif.com/forums.asp

Main office (UK, Europe):

The Software Centre, PO Box 2000, Nottingham, NG11 7GW, UK

Main:	(0115) 914 2000
Registration (UK only):	(0800) 376 1989
Sales (UK only):	(0800) 376 7070
Customer Service/ Technical Support:	http://www.support.serif.com/
General Fax:	(0115) 914 2020

North American office (US, Canada):

Serif Inc, The Software Center, 17 Hampshire Drive, Suites 1 & 2, Hudson, NH 03051, USA

Main:	(603) 889-8650
Registration:	(800) 794-6876
Sales:	(800) 489 6703
Customer Service/ Technical Support:	http://www.support.serif.com/
General Fax:	(603) 889-1127

International:

Please contact your local distributor/dealer. For further details, please contact us at one of our phone numbers above.

Credits

This Director's Guide, and the software described in it, is furnished under an end user License Agreement, which is included with the product. The agreement specifies the permitted and prohibited uses.

Trademarks

Serif is a registered trademark of Serif (Europe) Ltd.

MoviePlus is a registered trademark of Serif (Europe) Ltd.

All Serif product names are trademarks of Serif (Europe) Ltd.

HDV and the HDV logo are trademarks of Sony Corporation and Victor Company of Japan, Ltd.

Microsoft, Windows, and the Windows logo are registered trademarks of Microsoft Corporation. All other trademarks acknowledged.

PrimoSDK and Px Engine are trademarks of Sonic Solutions. All other trademarks are the property of their respective owners.

Blu-ray Disc and Blu-ray, and the logos are trademarks of the Blu-ray Disc Association.

AVCHD and the AVCHD logo are trademarks of Panasonic Corporation and Sony Corporation.

VST is a trademark of Steinberg Media Technologies GmbH.

Windows Vista and the Windows Vista Start button are trademarks or registered trademarks of Microsoft Corporation in the United States and/or other countries.

QuickTime is a trademark of Apple Computer, Inc., registered in the U.S. and other countries.

Copyrights

Digital Images ©2008 Hemera Technologies Inc. All Rights Reserved.

Digital Images ©2008 Jupiterimages Corporation, All Rights Reserved.

Digital Images ©2008 Jupiterimages France SAS, All Rights Reserved.

Content ©2008 Jupiterimages Corporation. All Rights Reserved.

Portions graphics import/export technology © LEAD Technologies, Inc.

Portions MPEG encoding technology © 1999/2000-2003 MainConcept AG.

Portions digital audio content © 2003-2005 Robert Bailey (http://www.a1freesoundeffects.com).

Introduction

Welcome to the MoviePlus X5 Director's Guide!

Whether you are new to MoviePlus or a seasoned movie maker, this guide offers content to help you get the best out of MoviePlus.

The Director's Guide offers tips on getting the best results from your raw video footage, a range of illustrated tutorials to familiarize yourself with the editing power of the Timeline, and full-colour previews of MoviePlus's Menu Templates. We hope you'll find this Director's Guide to be a valuable resource that you'll return to time and time again.

The Director's Guide is organized into the following chapters:

I: Shooting Guide

An overview giving suggestions for planning, shooting and editing your raw video footage.

2: Timeline Techniques

Illustrated, step-by-step training covering editing video content using the Timeline in MoviePlus.

3: Menu Templates

A reference gallery of the Menu Templates included with MoviePlus X5.

Contents

Shooting Guide

In the Shooting Guide section, we'll take you through the basics of movie making from the pre-filming, planning stage through to editing your raw footage. You'll learn the theory behind each of the steps, and some useful tips and tricks, which lead to a professionally produced video.

If you already have some footage and you want to skip the theory and start editing right away, check out the *Timeline Techniques* tutorials starting on p. 81. You can always come back to this section later.

Planning

The key to a great video is preparation, preparation, preparation!

Shooting a good video is not a simple process and there are many things to consider if you want to produce something that you'll enjoy watching at the end. Professional looking results require thought and planning. Before you begin filming, it's important to take some time to plan and prepare for your project. The following sections outline some of the fundamental principles that will help to make your project a success.

Decide on your story and how you want to tell it

It sounds obvious, but it's surprising how many people end up shooting aimlessly with no overall 'narrative thread' to hold the finished video or film together.

Telling your story

Think about the story you want to tell, and the way in which it will unfold. All good stories have a beginning, a middle and an end, even true ones! This is a basic principle, but one that distinguishes between boring haphazard footage that will confuse or send your audience to sleep, and a movie that will hold their attention.

Don't be afraid to use your 'stills' camera to record some of the important, but less exciting action. In MoviePlus it's easy to mix photos and videos to make a great looking movie!

The beginning:

These will be the 'preparation' shots. (These could even be photos.) For example:

- **Vacation** - shoot some footage of the family packing cases and some en route shots to your destination.

- **Birthday party** - film some of the party set up, maybe get some shots of making the party food, or even the hard work going in to writing the invitations! Get some shots of the guests arriving.

- **New activity** - say it's your child's first horse riding lesson, get there early and film them meeting the pony, tacking up and getting on for the first time.

- **Sports event** - try and get some shots of the time spent getting the equipment ready and capture the excitement and tension before the start of the competition. This could be an ideal time for a pre-competition interview!

The middle:

This is the main event! You'll want to film as much as possible (you can always cut the footage down later and remove any boring bits).

- **Vacation** - shoot any activities you do—playing in the sea, building sand castles,you might even catch some funny moments!—capture shots of the trips to new places or famous locations. Be sure to focus on the family, not just the amazing locations themselves!

- **Birthday party** - if you can't film the whole event, ensure you get shots of the entertainment, the games and activities, the "Happy Birthday" song, the blowing out of the candles, the present opening...

- **New activity** - if you can, shoot the entire activity (obviously, if it's an all day activity, just shoot the main action).

- **Sports event** - shoot the entire event, or at least the relevant parts of the competition (aka the ones where your competitor is taking part!).

The end:

- **Vacation** - at the end of the vacation, include footage of the return journey, children sleeping in the car, sunburned faces, waiting for the luggage at the carousel, etc.

- **Birthday party** - get some shots of the aftermath! You may want to end the tale with the present opening scenes, or even some nice shots of the birthday boy or girl. You could even get an interview!

- **New activity** - interview the star of the show! Find out how it went, did they enjoy it? Do they want to do it again? Get some after activity shots.

- **Sports event** - film the prize giving (especially if your family member has won a prize!), get a shot of the trophy, interview the winner, interview your competitor (even if they didn't win) and find out how they thought it went. Get some shots of packing away and cleaning up.

Storyboards and scripts

Your production will naturally fall into one of two types: **scripted** or **unscripted**.

Scripted:

This category includes movies, animated films and your garage band's latest music video. If you're filming an interview, the interviewer's questions will be scripted, while the answers obviously won't be. However, you can sometimes predict the type of response a question is likely to generate, which can be helpful in determining the flow of conversation and the way in which one question leads to another.

Unscripted:

This category includes documentary style films, news segments, and 'home videos' covering events such as weddings, vacations, birthday parties, and so on.

Always create a storyboard!

Whether your video will be scripted or unscripted, you should always create a storyboard. A storyboard is a visual script or plan of the scenes and scene changes in a series of video shots. While this step is an important one, many people ignore it and jump right into filming instead. So why is it so important?

- Creating a storyboard helps you to think about how you want your finished film to look, how the story should unfold, and what shots will best convey your story to the viewer.

- Storyboarding is especially useful for planning complex sequences of events, saving you from missing essential footage or shooting footage you can't use.

Your storyboard should include sketches of the most important scenes, notes about dialogue, sound effects, location, and so on.

For more information, see Storyboarding on p. 11.

Visit the location

Look for different or creative locations as these can really add impact to the shot. For many events (weddings, sports etc), you won't have much control over the location.

If you can, it's always a good idea to visit the location of your shoot beforehand so that you can plan your camera positions, maybe even take some trial footage. If you're filming your family vacation, however, you obviously won't be able to do this. Even so, you can still think about the location and the types of shots you think you'll need (again, this demonstrates the importance of creating a storyboard!)

Location checklist

The following list outlines the most important things to check on a location assessment:

- Is there enough light? If your shoot is taking place indoors, note the location of the windows. If you're shooting outside, think about the position of the sun at various times of the day.

- Is it quiet enough? Make a note of any background noise that might interfere with the audio recording.

- Is there enough space? Plan where you will position the camera to get the best shots, keeping in mind the background and light source. Remember, you may not be able to change where the action is taking place so it's up to you to find the best shooting position.

- If you need a power source, locate the nearest power outlet.

- In exterior locations, look for possible cover in case of adverse weather conditions (and/or invest in a rain cover for your equipment).

- Note how busy the site is at various times of the day.

- Do you need permission to film there? Are you on private property? If you need permission, always get it in writing.

- Locate the nearest car park—particularly important if you're using a lot of heavy equipment, or if you're using actors.

Storyboarding

Well planned videos look the most professional. Storyboarding is the process of creating a visual script, or draft, of the shots and scene changes in a video or film. This tutorial explains the storyboarding process, outlines the most common items found on a storyboard, and aims to provide guidelines for you to create your own.

Storyboards are invaluable when several people are working on a project together. A well-defined storyboard helps to ensure that everyone understands the goals of the project and how the video and audio footage should work together. However, if you're working alone, they also serve as visual reminders during the filming and editing stages. Remember, storyboards are not set in stone and can be revised as needed.

> You may find some sections too detailed for your purposes, or you may decide you need to include some additional elements in your storyboard.

Whatever type of production you're planning, bear in mind that the more detailed and specific your storyboard, generally the easier the production and post-production phases will be.

The storyboarding process is an important one for the following reasons:

- To deliver its message effectively, a video or film production needs to be well planned. Even a family event video will benefit from planning.

- Storyboarding helps you to think about how you want your finished film to look, how the story should unfold, and what shots will best convey your story to your audience.

- With your storyboard in place, you'll waste less time setting up shots because you'll know exactly what scenes you need to shoot, and where to shoot them from.

- Storyboarding is especially useful for planning complex sequences of events, saving you from shooting footage you can't use or missing footage that is essential to the plot.

Components

When creating a storyboard, think of your video as a story comprising various elements in a timeline. For each major scene, you should include information about who the subject is, what they are doing, where and why they are doing it, and so on.

If you know the location where you will be shooting, it's a good idea to sketch a rough plan view showing the placement of the camera, light source, people, and any other important features or props.

Include sketches of important scenes, along with scene descriptions, and notes about location, transitions, plot, dialogue, and sound effects.

Motocross race/Mallory   12 June 2010 / 10.30am

Shots of bike unloaded and last minute tweaks.   Wide establishing shot of course.   Establishing shot of riders. Then cut to medium-

Possibly stills. Dissolve to establishing shot.   Cut to start line.   wide shot with pan.

Scene 01 - approx 2-3 min   Scene 02 - 30s   Scene 03 - 5-15s

Draw arrows from one scene to the next where you are likely to makes edits. Write the type of transition you will use between each scene and/or colour-code the arrows. For information on transitions, see *Transitions* on p. 69.

Synopsis

At the top of your storyboard, write a short paragraph outlining the story or event that your video is going to capture. You could also include character profiles and any other issues related to the story.

Sketch

The example below shows a typical storyboard template. The blank 'boxes' are for sketching a rough representation of the main scenes that you want to capture during shooting. The lines below are for text.

Your sketches do not have to be detailed, (it's not an art contest!), but must be accurate enough so that you understand the type of shot required.

You might want to start by including a sketch of your establishing shot. This will set the scene for your audience and provide information about the location of your story.

You could then cut to a medium shot to introduce your subject. The idea is to create a sketch for each different shot that you want. If you want a close up, draw it! You can use arrows to depict camera panning and angles.

Establishing shot of riders. Then cut to medium-

wide shot with pan.

Scene 03 - 5-15s

You don't have to be an artist to create an effective storyboard—rough sketches of stick figures will do just as well.

While these examples vary stylistically, they all include the essential information. Try to include as much detail as possible about the scenes you want to shoot. Keep in mind also that a storyboard is a 'live document' and will change and evolve as your ideas develop.

Shot description

This section contains a description about what needs to be captured in the shot—specifically, anything that is difficult to explain in a single sketch.

Shots of bike unloaded and last minute tweaks.	Wide establishing shot of course.	Establishing shot of riders. Then cut to medium-
Possibly stills. Dissolve to establishing shot.	Cut to start line.	wide shot with pan.
Scene 01 - approx 2-3 min	Scene 02 - 30s	Scene 03 - 5-15s

For example, you might want to specify:

- The **estimated time** of take: How long (in seconds) you anticipate this segment will be. During shooting, this will help you to make sure that your long segments are long enough. During editing, it will help you determine which sections need to be shortened.

  In general, it's best to use longer shots for complex scenes and shorter shots for close ups.

- The **camera shot** required: Do you want this shot to be a close up, or an extreme close up? For information about different camera shots, see *Shot types* (p. 41).

- The **camera angle** required: For example, is this an aerial shot, an eye-level angle shot, a tilting shot? See *Shot angles* (p. 46).

Shot sequence number

You may think that the sequence of your shots is obvious. However, when you've added all the main elements of your storyboard, we suggest you assign each shot a sequence number.

As your ideas develop, you may decide to change the order of your shots. You'll find these sequence numbers invaluable when you come to edit your footage.

This is why professional movie makers use clapperboards noting the time, date and scene number before they start filming the scene!

Transitions

Identify your scene transitions—how you move from one shot to the next—in your storyboard. This will make the editing phase much easier, and will help you to determine if you have enough variation between shots.

For example, if you have the same type of shots following each other (a medium shot followed by another similar medium shot), you need to ensure that this won't be confusing for your audience. Don't use fancy transitions just because you can, use them when it will benefit the audience!

You should also compare the transition 'out' of one shot with the following transition 'in' of the next shot. 90% of your transitions should be straight cuts. Dissolves (from simple cross-fades to elaborate effects) imply a passing of time between shots. For information on transitions, see *Transitions* on p. 69.

Script

Make a note which sections need a script.

> ★ You may not need this section, but it's important to include it if you want a subject or narrator to follow a specific script during a particular scene.

If you're recording an interview, make a note of the questions to be asked and the responses you anticipate.

Audio

- **Primary audio -** As you capture your video footage, you can also simultaneously record your audio. If you're using an external microphone, make a note of when it should be used.

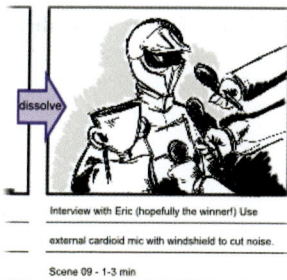

Interview with Eric (hopefully the winner!) Use
external cardioid mic with windshield to cut noise.
Scene 09 - 1-3 min

- **Background audio -** You should also note any scenes in which you don't want any sound recorded, and those where background audio is required. For example, at a track and field event, you might want to record the sound of the starter's gun, some crowd noise, applause, and so on.

- **Secondary audio -** If you want to add secondary audio to a scene during editing, make a note of it too. For example, in addition to the audio recorded during shooting, you might also want to include music, a voice-over, sound effects, or another audio track.

And that's all there is to it...

We've covered the major elements that are generally found on project storyboards. Keep in mind, however, that there are no strict rules for creating storyboards—each one will differ depending on the project it illustrates.

Practice Makes Perfect

Don't expect to get professional results with your camcorder the first time you use it! Filming techniques are varied and can take a while to perfect. It all comes down to experience. Go out and shoot as much as you can before filming an important event!

Get to know your equipment

Before you begin shooting, make sure you are familiar with your equipment (you might even want to read the manual!). Shoot at least a few hours of practice footage—in an ideal world, this should be as similar to the real thing as possible. For example, make sure that you attend the wedding rehearsal or the sports practice session. This will help you to foresee any problems that you might encounter, and you may also get some decent "pre-event" footage that you can include in your final movie!

Practice using your tripod and external microphone (if you're using one). You should be familiar with any equipment or techniques that you intend to use.

Using the camcorder

Most camcorders have built in image stabilisation. However, this is designed to correct slight hand shake and will not compensate for erratic movement! Camera shake also increases exponentially the more that you zoom into the shot.

Where possible always use a tripod or monopod. Not only will it improve the appearance of nearly all shots, it will also take the camera's weight! It's amazing how tired your arm starts to get after a while. Alternatively use a wall, a fence, a door frame, mini beanbag or any other stable structure for support.

You'll increase your stability by using the camcorder's hand or neck strap (or both). Hold the camcorder securely against your body and ideally use both hands. Keeping your arms bent and tucked in will also help reduce unwanted movement.

Experiment

Now is the time to experiment, try various lighting techniques to see the different effects you can achieve, but please, don't try new techniques on the day (at least, not until you have all of the footage you need!). New techniques take practice and experimentation. Note any techniques or shots you'd like to try, and then experiment at a time when it doesn't matter—not during a wedding video shoot, for example!

Rehearse difficult shots

Practice taking any difficult shots beforehand, especially those that require tricky camcorder techniques such as panning.

Use slow, smooth motion

A common mistake beginners make is to zoom in and out a lot. This can be very distracting for the audience.

While there are times when you might want to zoom, these types of shots should be kept to a minimum.

If you must pan a scene, move the camcorder smoothly and slowly (or follow some action to establish the scene, rather than just panning a scene with no action).

Avoid the 'firehose effect'—trying to capture the action in several different places by quickly jerking the camcorder around.

You'll find more tips on shooting moving subjects later in this section.

💡 If you need to capture a scene from different angles or with a different zoom setting, stop recording, move to a different position or change your zoom setting, and then continue shooting.

Use a dolly to shoot a moving subject

There will be times when you'll want to shoot a moving subject. These shots are particularly tricky if you're using a handheld camcorder as it's difficult to keep it level and steady.

Professionals use **dollies**—camcorder supports with wheels—for this purpose. Purpose-made dollies are very expensive, but you can make your own using virtually anything with wheels. For example, you could use a pushchair, wheelchair, or shopping trolley.

Make sure your 'dolly' moves smoothly and without noise, then secure your tripod and camcorder inside it. Before shooting, check the scene through the camcorder, and then adjust the tripod until you've achieved the shooting level you need.

You can now film your subjects in one of the following ways:

- By walking behind them.

- By walking beside them.

- By walking backwards, in front of them—be careful!

Focus

Your camcorder's automatic focus mode will work fine for shooting scenes where your subject is well and evenly lit, and in which there is contrast between the subject and the background. However, for all other situations, you'll need to be comfortable using manual focus.

Beginners often have problems when trying to shoot a night scene that contains bright objects, such as car headlights. Here, the automatic focus will centre on the car headlights as soon as they enter the scene, causing the focus of the subject to be lost. Many modern digital camcorders have a preset Night mode which will help you in these situations.

If you prefer to use the manual settings on your camcorder, the following technique will help you keep the subject of your night scene sharply in focus for the whole scene.

To shoot a low-light (night) scene:

1. Zoom in on your subject as tight as you can, viewing it through the LCD viewer.

2. Change to manual focus and adjust until your centre of interest is in sharp focus.

3. Zoom out from your subject, and then frame the scene using either the LCD viewer or the camcorder eyepiece.

4. Shoot the scene.

Once you've established the correct focus for your scene, don't be tempted to zoom in or out again—you'll lose focus if you do.

Exposure

The term exposure refers to the amount of light allowed through the camcorder lens. Getting this right often poses problems: too much light and the shot is over exposed; too little and it's under exposed.

Most camcorders have automatic exposure, which adjusts automatically according to the filming conditions. However, there will be times when the automatic exposure will not work correctly, for example, when filming a subject in heavy shade (under trees for example). In this case, the camcorder's automatic exposure adjusts to allow for the average lighting and therefore the detail of the subject is lost.

In these situations, it may be useful to explore some of your camcorder's preset modes. Many camcorders will provide you with a setting which will compensate for the shade without losing subject detail.

Alternatively, a useful way to get the correct exposure is to zoom in on your subject as tightly as possible to establish the correct exposure before shooting the scene. See *To shoot a low-light scene* on the previous page for more details.

Lux

The measurement of actual light available at a given distance, in any situation, is measured in units called 'lux' (symbolized lx). Your camcorder will have various settings to determine how much light it allows to enter the lens (usually by adjusting exposure and/or shutter speed). Experiment with these settings to see their effects on a shot.

Pre-filming Checklist

You don't want to be panicking and rushing around on the day of filming as there will be more chance of something going wrong. We recommend that you write a checklist of things to do before you leave. We've listed some of the essentials here, although not all of it will be relevant to every type of film.

If you cover everything on your checklist before filming, you should not miss a minute of the action!

Paperwork

* **script** (if needed) - print out enough copies for everyone who needs one and take a few spares as well.

* **storyboard** - take a copy of your storyboard along with you as a film shot checklist.

* **model/actor release forms** - if this is more than a home-movie, you'll need written permission from everyone who's going to appear in your film. Get them to sign a release form and keep it safe in a folder! You'll find form templates online.

* **location permission form** - if you're filming on private property, or using a listed (protected) location, ensure that you have written permission, especially if you intend to distribute your movie. You'll find form templates online.

* **'press' pass/event tickets** - at smaller events you may be able to talk to the organiser and obtain a 'press pass' giving you a prime location to get you closer to the action (for bigger events, this is usually reserved for actual members of the press). Don't forget, you may also need your ticket to get into the event!

- **insurance** - make sure you get adequate insurance for your equipment. Some events also require you to have adequate personal liability insurance.

Camcorder essentials

- **camcorder** - check it works! Also, make sure the lens is clean and is clear of spots, dirt and scratches.

- **camcorder accessories** - make sure the strap is attached and undamaged, and don't forget to pack a lens cleaning cloth or other dust remover.

- **storage media** - ensure that you have more storage (memory cards/sticks, blank DVDs, miniDV tapes or hard drive space) than you actually think you'll need. Ensure that they are formatted and ready to capture your video.

- **batteries** - charge all of your batteries, even the spares. Try not to let them get cold overnight as they won't last as long. Always take at least 1 spare battery, even for short shoots, in case one runs out or simply fails. Always buy good quality batteries.

- **'cue' point** - if you're using tape based media, and it's not a blank tape, ensure that the cue point (where you start recording from) is set correctly. If anyone has viewed previous footage on the tape, chances are that you could record over something important without this quick check!

Remember, other countries may use a lower voltage electrical supply so batteries will take longer to charge.

Important accessories

- **'stills' camera** - you'll always find one of these on a professional set! Taking still photos can provide great cutaway footage. You can also use it to capture some of the 'before' and 'after' moments. If you have a helper, get them to take the pictures while you film!

- **weather protection** - prepare for all weather and take protection for you and your equipment!

- **safety clothing** - in some locations you'll need to wear a hi-viz vest. Pack it with your camcorder gear.

- **tripod/monopod/dolly** - great for stable shots! Make sure that all of the clips or screws are tight and that nothing's missing.

- **microphones** - check all microphones are working before you take them out! If you need power, make sure batteries are fully charged and take spares. Don't forget to fit windshields or at least take them with you. If your microphones are wired, don't forget the leads!

- **external audio recording equipment** - if you're using external audio equipment, make sure that it's working, charged and that you pack any necessary leads.

- **headphones** - essential if you want to check that the recorded audio is clear.

💡 A disposable hand warmer can be used to keep batteries warm in very cold locations.

Useful extras

- **change for parking** - you may need it for the carpark!

- **duct tape** - it's amazing how versatile this stuff is! Use it for temporary repairs, securing wires... You never know when you might need it!

- **earplugs** - if you're filming at a loud location, for example a motor sports or music event, protect your hearing.

- **bin bags** - for rubbish but can also double up as a rain cover!

- **seat** - useful for outdoor events that involve a lot of standing around!

- **lunch!**

Setting Up the Shot

If you've done your planning well, this step should be easy! However, sometimes, the decision of where to place the camcorder has to be made on the day.

Before you shoot

You should take the following into consideration before you press record:

Consider your light source

Before you begin shooting your video, take a look at where the light is coming from.

To avoid turning your video subjects into shadows, shoot with the light source behind you, rather than behind your subject. Whenever possible, use natural light.

The automatic settings on your camcorder are often capable of correctly many light source problems. If necessary, try a few out until you find one you like and that works well.

Get a good, stable position

If you're using a tripod, set it up on level ground and make sure that it's not going to slip or fall over. Many tripods/monopods have a quick release system so that you can take some handheld shots as well. If you're using this, ensure that it's well attached to your camcorder.

If you're filming an outdoor event, ensure that you'll be comfortable where your standing and that there aren't any obstructions in your path. Looking through a viewfinder tends to restrict your view of oncoming objects!

Get a good, clear view

Visualise your shot before setting up, then choose your position relative to the background and where the action will take place. If you're filming a public event, try to ensure that you won't have anyone in the way, but be considerate and try not to block anyone else's view.

Set up your camcorder

Turn off the date/time stamp - You don't need to have the time and date displayed throughout your video! It will interfere with the editing process and reduce the visual impact of your movie. Digital media records the time and date into the exif data on the file. However, if you're using older media, record a shot of the time and date, clapperboard style, before you start!

Turn off camcorder effects - While it might be tempting to use your camcorder's built-in features (such as scene transition effects like auto fade), you should turn these off. Instead, concentrate on taking good quality footage—you can add any effects you want during editing.

Check the audio

The audio track is just as important to your final movie as the video footage. Before you start filming, check to make sure you're getting an audio feed (this is where your headphones come in!)

If you're going to use the camcorders recorded audio (if you don't intend to replace it while editing), check the sound regularly, ideally monitor it with headphones while you are filming. This way you'll know the instant there is a problem or extraneous background noises that might be distracting.

For more information and tips on recording sound, see the "Audio" section starting on p. 49.

Shoot everything!

When you start to shoot, capture everything you can. You can edit as much as you want later, but it's better to have lots of footage to choose from.

Press Record before the shot begins - Some camcorders don't start to record the instant you press the Record button, so you should allow a couple of seconds extra. To make sure you capture everything, start shooting about 20 seconds or so before the shot really begins.

Use autofocus carefully - Autofocus is useful for giving certain images a crisp effect. It's not perfect though and can be easily fooled in certain conditions, such as footage in which your subjects are moving, when there's little contrast between subject and background, or when filming through elements such as windows, fences, trees, etc. For maximum control you should turn it off and set your focus manually instead. Make sure you practise this technique beforehand!

Allow time for the scene to end - After you've finished recording, wait a second or two before you end the scene, especially if you need to move to change location. This way you'll ensure that your shots don't end with distracting jerky movement.

During filming -

- Check battery levels on a regular basis as you don't want them to run out during the important action.

- Check the lens in adverse conditions to ensure it's still clean and fog free.

- Check the footage occasionally to ensure that it's ok and your focus, exposure and shot angle are still good.

- Try not to use the live LCD screen available on many digital camcorders, they tend to drain the battery super fast!

- Check that any peripherals haven't come loose (tripod, straps etc.), especially if you're moving around a lot.

Record plenty of B-roll - There are a several reasons why you should shoot more raw footage than you think you need for a particular project. To begin with, you'll have more material to work with during the editing phase. You'll also be able to build a library of 'stock' footage that you can use in other projects.

Building your stock library

Particularly useful are non-specific shots that you can use in any video—sunsets, landscapes, seascapes, and so on. Such shots are great for transitions, or to 'set the scene.'

Composition and Framing

Before you start shooting, take a good look at your shot. Do you have everything that you want in the shot? Is the shot framed well? The following tips will help you create balanced, professional-looking footage.

Create a balanced composition

Composition is as important in movies as it is in still photos. Look at the shapes and the colours in the shot. They should create a balanced picture and draw attention to the subject, rather than drawing the eye away from it. If you're not happy with the way your shot is set up, try taking it from another position or angle.

Choose the backdrop carefully - A good background should be neutral or should compliment the video subject; it should not overwhelm it or distract from it. Avoid background clutter and objects that could merge with your subject to create distracting effects—such as a tree that appears to 'grow' out of a person's head, or people waving and jumping around trying to get on camera!

Rule of Thirds - When setting up a composition, use the rule of thirds to create space, interest and balance in your shots. This rule states that if you divide your frame roughly into thirds, horizontally and vertically, any points where those lines intersect is a good place to position your main subject.

Unless you're zoomed in close, placing your subject in the centre of the shot does not create interest.

Watch for headroom, looking room, and lead space -These terms refer to the amount of room in the frame which is purposely left empty.

- **Headroom** is the amount of space between the top of the subject's head and the top of the frame. Leaving too much headroom wastes frame space and makes your subject appear to be sinking. In a close up, too little headroom draws the viewer's eye to the chin and neck, rather than the eyes.

- **Looking room** is the amount of space left in the direction the subject is looking. When shooting one person talking to another—the person on the left should be framed to the left of centre, the other person to the right. If you're shooting a subject who is talking directly to camcorder—place the subject to the left or right of centre. (This is related to the Rule of Thirds principle.)

- **Lead space** refers to the space in front of a moving subject, for example a person walking or a moving vehicle. This may also be referred to as **nose room**, or **look space**. Without adequate lead space, the frame will look awkward.

Framing

Make sure your subjects are looking into the frame – This is related to **Lead Space**. Unless the subject is naturally passing through the frame, you should always try to film them so that they appear to be looking or moving towards the centre of the frame. If they don't, your viewers will begin to feel a little uncomfortable as they'll feel as though they're "missing something".

Perspective - Use perspective creatively to draw your audience into an image. It's a great way to change or enhance the mood. See *Shot Angles* on p. 46 for inspiration.

'Natural frames' - Shoot your subjects inside frames—for example, a building through an archway, a person in a doorway, your subject framed by the branches of a tree.

Shot Types and Angles

When shooting video footage, there are some basic principles that can make a big difference and will help you to produce better quality raw footage and ultimately, professional-looking results. The following section provides some guidelines.

Rather than filming in one continuous take, divide the scene up into separate shots. Any activity can be broken down into individual moments in time. The secret of good video shooting is being able to identify these, and thus divide a complete action into a series of separate shots.

During the editing phase, you can decide which shots to keep and which ones to discard.

Shot types

To create an interesting video, you need to include a variety of different types of shots. Shots are commonly divided up into the following categories:

Close Ups

Close ups convey the detail and emotion to the viewer. They vary from the real extreme close up to the standard head and shoulders shot.

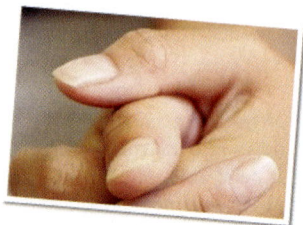

Extreme close up (ECU) - Any shot that zooms in very close to a particular part of a subject is known as an extreme close up. They vary considerably but usually focus on a particular part of a person—the face, mouth, eyes, hands, etc—object, or animal. These shots can create a feeling of intimacy in your video, and to convey a mood or emotion. These shots are very intense, so use them sparingly. The ECU is too close to show general reactions or emotion except in very dramatic scenes. They are generally preceded, and followed, by a wider shot.

Close up (CU) - Close up shots typically contain just the face and shoulders of a subject, with a little head room above. This prevents 'floating head syndrome' as the shoulders suggest to the brain that there is a body below! These shots are the most common of all as they can convey a real sense of emotion and help the audience to connect with the subject.

Profiles - This is a full side-on view of a subject (where you can only see one eye). You should try to avoid this type of shot when shooting people as it will make the viewer feel uncomfortable. However, it can be a useful shot when filming action.

Medium Shots

Medium shots (or mid shots) typically frame subjects from the waist up. These shots help to show people in the context of the background. They are used extensively in film production as they portray the audience's everyday perception of people.

Medium shot (MS) - The 'waist up' medium shot is ideal when the subject is speaking or delivering information and the fine detail isn't needed. It's also useful when people are gesturing with their arms. The problem with medium shots is that they don't show as much detail as a close up, but they introduce more of the background. This can be distracting.

Two-shot or three-shot (2-S or 3-S) - Often medium or wide shots, these are shots of two or three people in one scene. They are often used in interviews and are also good for establishing a relationship between subjects.

Long (Wide) Shots

A long shot shows a great deal of background, be it the set, the landscape or the venue. Long shots are essential to establish the scene for the viewer and to put the rest of the film into context. This is why they are also known as **establishing shots**. Watch carefully, and you'll see that almost every TV program or movie starts with a long shot, and then uses them whenever the scene changes. After the long shot, you'll see mostly close ups.

Extreme wide shot (EWS) - Extreme wide shots are far removed from the subject and often shot with a wide-angle lens. They may show the subject in the distance, but the emphasis is more on showing the subject in his or her environment.

Wide shot (WS) - Wide shots (also known as long shots) provide an overall view of the whole scene. If the shot contains a person, the whole body is shown.

Creative Shots

Creative shots can fall into the close up, medium or long shot category. They provide a different perspective for your viewer. They can be really effective but the more unusual viewpoints should be used sparingly.

Over-the-shoulder shot (OSS) - These shots look at the subject from behind a person. They show the back of a person's head (often cutting off the frame just behind the ear) and sometimes one shoulder.

Reaction shot - Also known as noddy shots, these shots show a person's face listening or reacting to something. Reaction shots are common in interviews and are also often used to cut into a sequence and hide jump cuts.

Point of view shot (POV) - Also called a subjective shot. The camcorder adopts the perspective of a character. We see what a character sees and therefore identify with him/her. The person whose point of view it is should never be seen in the shot. These shots are often used to add drama in chase scenes.

Cutaway (CA) - Placed between the main shots, a cutaway is usually of something other than the current action. These shots are used as transitions between main shots, or to add interest or information. For example, a typical CA shot could be a close up of the subject's mouth or hands—also known as a cut-in (CI), or a shot of an entirely different subject.

Shot angles

The shot angle is the level from which you look at your subject through the camcorder.

As a general rule, shoot people at (their) head height.

Try to vary the shot angle as much as possible as you may find an unusual view that will add interest to your movie. You're also guaranteed to end up with a greater variety of footage to work with when editing.

Eye-level angle - Because this is the perspective most familiar to us, the eye-level angle is one of the most commonly used shots. If you want to shoot at this angle, however, bear in mind that 'eye-level' refers to your subject's eye level—not yours.

High angle - In these shots, the camcorder looks down on the subject making it appear smaller and less important. High angle shots are often used to make a person appear vulnerable.

Low angle - In low angle shots, the camcorder looks up at the subject. Use these shots when you want to make your subject appear larger, imposing, or more important to the viewer.

Don't just stick to the basic shot angles though. Be adventurous and experiment with shot angles and perspective...

Tilting shot - Experiment with panning in the vertical plane instead of the horizontal.

Forward/backward tracking shot - Try shooting a moving subject from behind, or when they are coming towards you.

When shooting subjects that are close to the ground, get down on the same level.

If you're crouching, use your knee to balance the camcorder; for very low shots, lie on the ground and use your elbows for support. Most camcorders have eyepieces that you can adjust for easier viewing angles.

If your subject is a child, get down on their level; the results will be much more effective than filming from yours.

Improving Audio Quality

Although you may not have realised it, the most important aspect of a movie or video is its soundtrack. The power of good quality audio is its ability to go unnoticed! However, poor quality audio is picked up immediately and can make your video unwatchable. It's actually better to have no audio at all!

If you've ever watched a home movie (and who hasn't?) you'll probably have noticed that the sound of people speaking is often a little tinny, and the clearest sounds come from the person behind the camera or even the camera itself!

In this section, we'll have a quick look at why you get poor audio, and more importantly, what you can do to improve your own video audio.

The three top tips to improve the audio on a home movie are:

- Replace poor audio with a different backing track.

- Use an external microphone to record the audio.

- Use headphones to listen to the audio when recording.

Replacing the audio

If your recorded audio is of really poor quality, one of the easiest things you can do is to replace the entire audio track with a new one. You could either use a piece of music, or you could record a new audio voiceover track.

Replacing the audio during the editing process is extremely easy with MoviePlus. It also gives you much more freedom when editing your video and cutting different scenes together as you don't need to worry about audio continuity.

Using an external microphone

If you need high quality audio that matches your movie, then you should really use a decent quality external microphone. (For information on the types of microphone available, see *Microphones* on p. 57).

Most consumer camcorders have a 3.5mm stereo jack for attaching an external mic, so you'll need a mic/lead combination that will match. (Professional camcorders generally use an XLR jack.) Most microphones plug directly into the camera using a long lead (automatically disconnecting the onboard microphone). However, some microphones also have a wireless version that works with a transmitter.

Common microphones for filming applications

To help you choose a microphone, we've listed a few common ones alongside their basic usage. With any type of microphone, if you can, wear decent headphones so that you can monitor the audio quality while you film.

Most types of microphones are available in wired and wireless versions. Wired camcorder microphones connect directly into your camera. Wireless microphones come with a receiver and a transmitter. The transmitter is connected to the microphone, and the receiver is connected to your camcorder. Wireless microphones allow you much more freedom when recording as you aren't limited by the length of lead! However, they are also much more expensive than wired microphones, and you have still have to consider range, signal interference and battery power.

On-camera microphones

Most cameras have a built-in microphone. These are normally *electret condenser* microphones and are usually *omnidirectional*. The closer the sound source, the clearer it will be. If you have to use the on-camera microphone, where possible get in close to your subject to reduce the interference from background noise (including the camera operator and even the sound of the camera itself!). Handling noise can be reduced by using a tripod while filming (this will also improve your video quality!).

Handheld microphones

The archetypal microphone! These dynamic microphones are multipurpose, rugged and perform well in all environments. If you want good sound on a tight budget, you won't go far wrong by adding a good dynamic microphone to your arsenal. They tend to have a *cardioid* pattern (see p. 59) and eliminate a lot of unwanted noise from the surrounding area.

Some handheld microphones are the condenser type. These tend to be used in conjunction with a stand. If you're only recording narration, condenser microphones tend to have a warmer sound.

The downside with handheld microphones is that as they have to be close to the sound source, they can lend your videos a 'news' like feel if you're not recording some sort of performance. However, they do make great microphones when recording voice in a studio (or in front of your PC).

Lavalier microphones

Lavalier microphones are also known as 'tie-clip' or 'lapel' microphones as they are miniature microphones that are generally worn on the clothing. People tend to feel less self-conscious as they often forget that they're wearing a microphone! However, the microphone must be placed carefully as they can be susceptible to noise from being rubbed by material. Lavalier microphones come in wired and wireless versions and can make a great difference to your recording.

Headset microphones

Headset microphones are ideal for people who move around a lot as the microphone is always kept at the correct distance from the mouth. They are commonly worn by sports presenters, stage performers and fitness instructors. You can find a headset to suit all budgets, wired and wireless versions, and some even plug directly into the PC if you're recording video narratives.

Shotgun microphones

Shotgun microphones are the ones you'll most often see when people are filming. They are normally attached to a boom pole and covered in a fur windshield. As these *supercardioid* microphones are effective at distance and super-directional, they can be used to get clear audio from the talent or when recording sounds from nature.

If you don't have a dedicated soundman (and you probably won't!) it is possible to attach a shotgun microphone to some camcorders. While this isn't ideal, it will still significantly improve the overall sound compared to the built-in microphone.

Indispensable accessories

The following are the accessories that we'd class as almost indispensable!

Pop shields

One of the best accessories you can use when recording in a studio environment (or in front of your computer) is a pop shield. When we speak, we expel air from our mouths. Words starting with 'B' or 'P' (plosives) cause bursts of air to be released. These cause the pop and thump sounds from a microphone.

A pop shield is a screen of nylon, or metal mesh material that is stretched over a circular frame. The material prevents the plosives from reaching the microphone, but isn't thick enough to distort the sound. To be effective, the pop shield must be placed a couple of inches in front of the microphone capsule as it needs a gap of still air to be effective.

Windshields

Windshields are an essential addition to any microphone when filming outside. Not only do they help to reduce unwanted wind noise, they also reduce breath noise and help to protect the microphone from the elements. Windshields come in two types, foam and fur.

Foam windshields are the most common type and are often supplied when you buy the microphone. If not, most manufacturers provide them as an optional accessory. The foam will filter out a light breeze when filming outdoors.

Fur windshields are made with long, synthetic fur (usually grey in colour) and are normally used to cover shotgun microphones when filming outdoors. They are used in windy conditions and can reduce wind noise by up to 18dB in gusts of 22mph! The long fibres ensure that the only sound eliminated is wind noise.

Boom pole/stand

If your not using a lavalier or headset microphone, then you may want to use a boom pole or stand. They come in multiple sizes for different purposes and ensure that you have total handsfree operation. A microphone and boom pole can also be used to extend your reach if you need to get the microphone closer to the action.

Tripod/Monopod

Hold your camcorder steady with a tripod or monopod. Keeping the camcorder still will not only reduce unwanted handling noise, but it will also improve your picture quality! (You could also use a bean bag to protect your camera when using a wall or the floor!)

Microphones

When you decide to invest in a microphone you'll come across a whole new world of terms and technical jargon. However, there are so many types, sizes and shapes, where do you start? Microphones have several characteristics; type, polar pattern, frequency response and size. Understanding these makes it a lot easier to choose the right microphone for the job. Hopefully, this guide will help you!

Dynamic or Condenser?

Most microphones used in sound recording for video are either **dynamic** or **condenser** types.

Dynamic microphones are your general, hand-held microphones that you see on stage and for outdoor interviews, especially in loud, hostile environments. They work via electromagnetic induction, using a wire coil and a magnet to create the audio signal. This makes them really resilient to knocks, temperature, moisture and to high volume levels that could seriously damage condenser microphones. What's more, they don't require external power to work. However, if you need to record only in a studio environment, record really soft sounds, or if you need something a little less obtrusive, then you may need to look at a condenser microphone.

Condenser microphones are probably the most common type of microphone and come in many shapes and sizes. They use a capacitor to convert acoustical energy into electrical energy. This means that they need external power (either via an internal battery or via 'phantom' power, i.e., power derived from another source such as the camcorder itself).

Condenser microphones have a faster frequency response and are more sensitive to sound. As a result, they give a smooth, natural sound and are ideally suited to a studio environment or film production. However, they are also much more delicate and can distort or even break when exposed to high volumes! Unless they are the expensive RF type, condenser microphones are highly susceptible to condensation.

Electret condenser microphones use a special type of capacitor that remains permanently charged. This means that, unless they include a pre-amplifier, they don't require any external power. Electret microphones are often found in computers, mobile phones and "hands-free" kits.

Choosing a microphone

Choosing a microphone can be a complicated affair. Most consumer camcorders have a 3.5mm stereo jack for attaching an external mic, so you'll need a mic/lead combination that will match. (Professional camcorders generally use an XLR jack.) Microphones vary in price, so you'll need to buy the best one to suit your budget. It's worth noting that wired microphones generally cost a lot less than wireless versions. It's up to you to do some research to find the one that best suits your needs.

The type of microphone you'll need to buy will largely depend on the type of video you'll be shooting, and the type of audio you need e.g., narration, music, , commentary, conversation... Different microphones pick up sound from different directions—the **microphone polar pattern**. The polar pattern is normally listed under the technical specifications that come with the microphone. Knowing a little about your chosen microphone will help you to get the best from it.

Microphone polar patterns

Different microphones pick up sound from different directions—the microphone polar pattern. This means that your choice of microphone can be tailored to a specific situation.

There are essentially five main types of polar pattern.

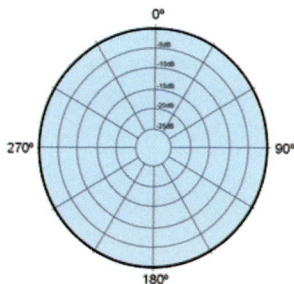

Omnidirectional

These pick up sound equally from all directions. They produce a very natural sound and the microphone does not have to be aimed specifically. This is most useful when your sound source is frequently moving around. This is why lavalier microphones are omnidirectional. The disadvantage is that undesired sound sources may also be picked up.

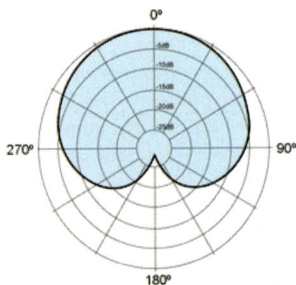

Cardioid

Microphones with this pattern pick up the vast majority of sound from the front and a reasonable amount from the sides. Very little, however, is picked up from behind. As a result, you can point this mic at the sound you want to pick up. This is probably the most commonly used pattern you will come across as it is very versatile and can be used in practically all situations.

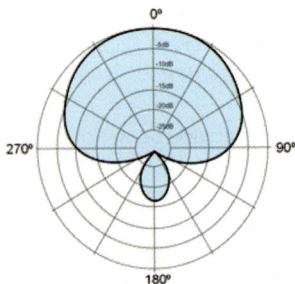

Hypercardioid

These have a similar pattern to caridioid but the response from the sides (referred to as off-axis) is less. This makes it more directional than the Cardioid. Hypercardioid microphones are used when isolation between sound sources is important. They are less sensitive to off-axis sounds and will not pick up near-by sources as easily. Due to their more directional nature, they are less likely to cause feedback.

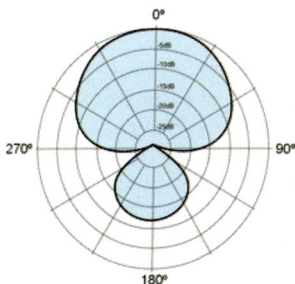

Supercardioid or Shotgun

Shotgun microphones have a very tight pickup pattern and are highly directional. (Note that they will pick up some sound from directly behind the microphone.) They are used primarily to pick up sounds from a distance. Common uses are in broadcast/film recording work where the mic can be held or suspended 'off-camera' and in the theatre for picking up actors on stage without having to individually mic them all. Due to the sensitivity of these microphones, they are all condensers and, as such, require a phantom power supply.

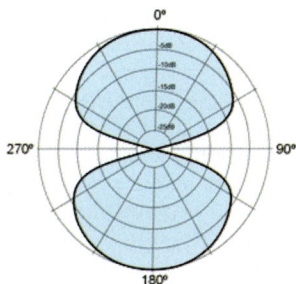

Figure-of-8 (Bi-directional)

These pick up sound from the front and rear of the microphone but not the sides. They are mostly used when making stereo recordings or when doing across-table interviews.

Audio Tips and Tricks

The following tips will help you get the most out of your audio recordings.

- **Test your equipment before you leave!** It's better to find out a microphone isn't working when you're at home than on location.

- **Use earphones.** Take a pair of earphones with you so you can listen to the sounds you're capturing.

- **Get up close.** If you're using a built-in microphone, to get the clearest possible audio and reduce unwanted background noise, get as close as possible to your subject (about three feet away is best if you want to get a good head and shoulders shot). Don't forget that the microphone will also capture any noise you make.

- **Use an external microphone.** Position the microphone according to its type. Dynamic microphones should be approximately six inches from the sound source, other types will vary. Make sure that any condenser microphones have suitable power and are working. Ideally use stands and/or boom poles where appropriate.

- **Use pop filters and/or windshields.** When recording outside, always use a windshield. You could even make your own furry windshield for the built-in microphone! Use a pop filter for all studio recording.

Commercially available windshields and pop filters vary in price. Windshields, can be made from foam or fake fur available from craft stores (especially useful for your built-in microphone!). Pop filters can be made by stretching nylon tights or stockings over a loop—you could use an embroidery hoop (4-6 inches depending on mic size) or a bent wire coat hanger. You could even use a kitchen sieve! A quick search on the internet will provide all of the DIY information you need.

- **Use a tripod.** This will reduce unwanted handling noise.

- **Eliminate unnecessary background noise** before you start recording. If you don't, you're likely to get different background sound with each shot.

- **Record additional audio.** Record relevant background noise to add to your audio tracks. During editing, you can then use these tracks to create continuity between shots.

- **Audio is 50% of your film!** Be aware of the impact of music and sound effects on your video footage. Choose carefully to reflect the feeling and pace of your shots.

- **Record everything!** When recording live performances, make sure you record the entire piece of music or stage dialog. During the editing phase, you can then select your best video shots and lay them against this continuous soundtrack.

- **Do a trial run** to identify any distortion and determine consistent sound levels from your subjects and background sources. Do a test, then play it back on your earphones.

- **Reduce ambient noise.** Close doors and windows and turn off any air conditioning units. If you're recording narration, ideally record in a corner of the room, in an area that is 'insulated' with absorbent material of some kind (you can buy special screens or simply use foam, blankets, curtains, carpet, mattresses, even egg boxes!).

Editing

Even if you have bought the best equipment and captured some great video and audio footage, all your efforts will be wasted if you make the wrong editing decisions! In this section we'll set you on the right track and help you achieve results you can be proud of.

The video editing process is very similar to putting together any type of presentation—the editor 'cuts and pastes' various video and audio segments together, and adds effects and titles where necessary. Video editing requires both artistic and technical skills. It also requires a lot of time—and this applies to both the novice and professional editor.

- **Artistic skills** - The artistic process involves deciding what elements to keep, delete, or combine so that they come together in a coherent and visually pleasing manner.

- **Technical skills** - The technical process consists of knowing how to use MoviePlus X5 to achieve your artistic goals.

> You should consider the editing phase even as you're filming your video. This will help you to make the right decisions about what to shoot, and where and how to shoot it. Aim to film each shot from more than one angle. This will give you plenty of options when you come to edit your movie.

Follow the pro tips!

There's nothing wrong with taking inspiration from professional productions. Notice how establishing shots are used, what transitions are most effective, and how clips are put together—sometimes so seamlessly that you hardly notice, and at other times quite dramatically.

1. Keep it short

Audiences have a limited attention span. Hold their interest by keeping your production 'tight':

- It only takes a few seconds for the viewer to absorb and understand a static shot so these clips should be very short (1-2s max).

- Longer clips should be just long enough to depict all the action.

- Don't drag it out! Most shots shouldn't be longer than 15-20s without a cut to a different shot. However, this doesn't have to effect the audio track! There are always exceptions to the rule.

2. Keep it moving

The fun is in the action. Cut and cut again. MoviePlus makes it easy for you to cut out the boring bits—the extra two minutes it takes your child to open each Christmas presents, or the entire race. Try to create short, exciting sequences!

3. Tell a story

When assembling your video clips, your goal is to build them into a coherent story or sequence of events. (See *Continuity* on p. 73.) They don't necessarily have to follow in the chronological order in which they were shot!

A tried and tested method is to start with an establishing shot to set the scene, and then move on to the action scenes. The clips should be ordered logically and should build towards a climax. Ideally, try to cut different types of shot together—vary the shot type and camera angle (but don't cross the line!).

4. Maintain pace and style

When you planned and shot your video, you should also have thought about how you wanted your finished production to look (remember the *storyboard*?). The pace and style will be affected by the visual and audio content, as well as the length of your shots and the way in which you move from one clip to the next.

5. Careful cuts

Cuts within a scene should be virtually seamless and the viewer should hardly be aware of them. With careful editing, you can cut all types of footage together to make a coherent video.

This is easier said than done. However, you'll find that the more editing you do, the better your cutting technique will become. Cuts appear more natural if they have a purpose, for example, cutting from one scene to the next to provide more information about the story or location (you can use different camera angles to do this). Similarly, switching between two characters involved in a conversation will also appear natural.

Vary shot lengths - Your movie will be more interesting if you vary your shot lengths. For example, use longer shots for establishing shots (to set the scene) and for complex shots such as a busy street scene; use shorter shots for close ups and reaction shots.

If you can't make perfectly matched shots, insert some B-roll!

B-roll is the footage that sets the scene, reveals detail and enhances your story. It's one of the most commonly used ways of covering mis-matched cuts and smoothing transitions.

Transitions

MoviePlus provides a wide selection of transition effects, ranging from simple fades to more complex geometric designs. As a beginner, you may be tempted to use them liberally throughout your project. However, if your aim is to create a professional looking video, avoid temptation and stick to the basics.

Do some research—you'll find that you hardly ever see fancy transitions in movies or television shows.

The following list describes the simplest and most common transition methods used.

The cut

The cut isn't really a transition at all, but simply involves replacing one shot with another. Cuts are fast and efficient. They maintain continuity because they mimic the way we look at things in real life—our line of vision quickly jumps from one thing to the next. For this reason, cuts are the best way to keep the action rolling at a good pace (so timing is key). Fancier transitions can be distracting and slow down the pace. Cuts are used 90% of the time in every professional production!

Don't be afraid to mix live footage with photos! They can make great cut scenes and add to the video.

The dissolve (cross-fade)

This is when a shot gradually fades between clips, or to/from a single colour, usually black or white (often at the start or end of a movie). It's a useful (and often used) transition, and in movies typically occurs when the story changes locations.

The speed of the fades indicates the importance of the change in time and/or location between scenes.

A slower fade with more time spent on black indicates a more significant end/beginning. A quick fade to/from black might indicate a time lapse of a few minutes or hours, whereas a long fade indicates a much bigger change.

The wipe

This effect is more obvious than the fade and the viewer is supposed to notice it. The wipe denotes a major change in location or time. It might also be used to show a main character changing over time, wiping between clips of him or her at various points in time.

For details on working with transitions and effects in MoviePlus, see MoviePlus Help or the **How To** pane.

Don't overdo transition effects

- A transition is the process of changing from one shot to the next.

- Professional productions generally stick to the more standard transition types and don't jump from one type to another.

- Unless you're really comfortable with the editing process, it's best to stick with the smooth and simple cut, dissolve, and fade to black or from black. (For more on transitions, see p. 16.)

As you play your video and audio footage, you'll notice some obvious 'natural' cutting points. For example, a person getting up from a chair during a close up shot, a drink being put down on a table, or even a simple head turn. In audio footage, a cut may occur when an sound is heard off-camera—a doorbell ringing, a person laughing, a car engine starting up, and so on.

Continuity

When you put your video together, it's important to maintain the illusion of continuity. We've all noticed glaringly obvious mistakes in movies—objects changing hands in between scenes, drink glasses full, empty and then full again, the list is endless. However, continuity isn't just about props, it's also about making your video flow from scene to scene in a seamless way. Continuity is as important in home movies as it is in the latest blockbuster!

Although we're discussing continuity as part of the editing process, you should also consider it while filming. If, as we've suggested before, you've filmed 'everything', maintaining continuity should be a relatively easy exercise.

What is a cut?

A cut is essentially a point (transition) in the video where you go from one scene or shot to another. In the not too distant past, editors used to actually cut the film strip to split it from the next section, and the terms have stayed with us into the digital revolution.

For more detail on transitions, see *Transitions* on p. 69.

Avoid jump cuts

If you place two shots together that are too similar, but not seamless, it can have a jarring effect on the viewer. This is particularly the case when the subject is moving. If two shots filmed a few seconds apart are added together, it can make your subject appear as though they are stuttering and jumping through time.

If you need to put two scenes together that would result in a jump cut, you should use a cutaway showing something different in between the shots. This distracts the viewer's attention enough for the mind to fill in the movement that they haven't actually seen. You'll see this method all of the time in on tv and in movies, and it's why you see a shot of the reporter nodding during a news report!

It's much better to place two obviously different shots together. However, to make them appear as though they are following in sequence, you must still abide by a few continuity rules!

Cut on the action

If you're cutting between a wide shot and a close up shot that involves someone moving from one position to another, you'll need to make a cut at some point. Motion distracts the eye from noticing editing cuts. The best place to make the cut is 'on the action' i.e., during the movement from one position to the next.

Don't cross the line!

Known as the '180 degree rule,' this standard rule of filmmaking states that to maintain consistent screen direction, the camcorder should always stay on one side of the **"axis of action"** (**A**).

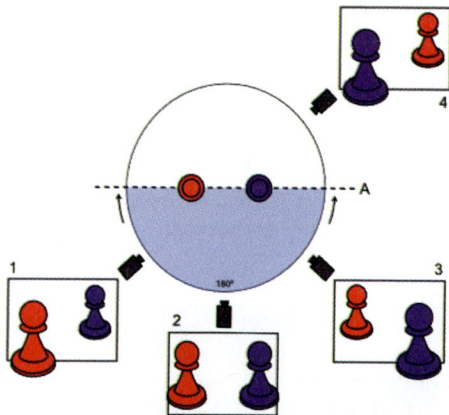

The illustration shows the effect of the 180 degree rule. The camera can film anywhere along the 180 degree divide line (the shaded area). Any shots used will always make sense to the viewer as the 'action' is always flowing in the same direction (**1, 2, 3**). However, if you film from the opposite side of the line (**4**) the orientation changes. This change of orientation would appear strange and confusing to the viewer and the effect is even worse when the subject is moving.

To avoid making this mistake, you should try to set up your scene and subjects so that you can shoot all from the same side. Imagine a line cutting through the middle of the scene—the camcorder should never cross this line.

Shooting the action

When shooting a scene showing a subject moving from left to right, the imaginary line runs across the scene on the subject's left side. If you were to move to the other side of the line and continue to shoot, the scene would be reversed and your subject would now be walking from right to left. This is really important to bear this in mind if you are cutting to different angles!

"But, I have to cross the line!"

There are some situations in which crossing the line is unavoidable. In these cases, take a shot right on the 'line' itself and then use this as a transition to 'guide' your audience to the new orientation.

Remember, if you have to cross the line:

- Use a moving shot that shows the crossing of the axis of action.
  or -

- Indicate on screen that a shot is a "Reverse Angle" as is done in sporting events.

> Incidentally, if there is a change in direction, ensure that you don't quickly cut between scenes. Allow your subject to exit the frame, and then re-enter it from the new direction.

Editing in MoviePlus

MoviePlus has two modes, Timeline (the default mode for editing) and Storyboard (especially useful for slideshows). When you start each new project, the first few steps are pretty much the same regardless of which mode you choose to use.

At the start of a new project:

1.   Add all your clips to the **Media** pane.

2.   Select each of your clips in turn and trim any unwanted pieces.

3.   Drag the clips you want to use onto the storyboard or timeline, in the sequence you prefer.

(For instructions on how to do this, see the **How To** pane.)

> 💡 If your captured footage is very big, you might prefer to do some editing before you import into MoviePlus.

Storyboard mode

For simple projects, especially if you are creating photo slideshows, the storyboard is all you need to quickly create a movie. Simply drag clips, photos, and background music tracks onto the storyboard from the **Media** pane.

You can reorder your clips; trim away unwanted portions; add text, transitions, and special effects; and finally share your finished movie in a variety of popular formats.

The **How To** pane covers the Storyboard mode in detail.

Timeline mode

For more advanced projects, the timeline offers all the manual editing operations that traditional film editors require.

For example, you can work with multiple video and audio tracks; add and edit envelopes; apply masks and overlays, and more.

For detailed information on working in Timeline mode, see MoviePlus Help. For step-by-step instructions on how to create specific effects, see the tutorials, "*Timeline Techniques*."

Timeline Techniques

In the Timeline Techniques section, we'll show you how to use MoviePlus X5 to edited your raw footage into a movie with stunning visuals and sounds. You'll learn how to manipulate clips on the Timeline using a variety of techniques used by professionals.

To improve your raw footage for future projects, check out the wealth of information and tips in the *Shooting Guide* starting on p. 1.

Trimming and Splitting

Trimming and splitting are cutting room floor techniques that will tidy up your video clips quickly and easily. Trimming removes unwanted frames from the start or end of a clip; splitting allows you 'cut' a clip into smaller sections, without losing any frames in the process. You will also need to combine trimming and splitting if you want to use fancy slow motion effects on sections of your video!

By the end of this tutorial you will be able to:

- Trim a clip.

- Split a clip.

Let's begin...

- Open a new project in timeline mode and then import a video clip to the **Media** pane **Project** tab.

Trimming

Whatever project you're working on, we suggest that you try to 'shoot everything.' If you follow this advice, you'll have lots of footage to choose from during the editing process. You'll also have footage that you won't want to include in your finished movie.

For example, clips seldom begin or end exactly where you'd like; there may be extra frames at the beginning or end, or you may want to use a short section from the middle of the clip. The solution is to trim the clip—adjusting its in-point and/or out-point to include just the piece you want.

How you trim your clip really depends on the clip itself. We'll look at two methods. Try them out and see which one works best for you.

To trim a clip in the Trim dialog:

1. In the **Media** pane, select a clip and click ✐ **Trim**. The **Trim** dialog opens and displays the first frame of the clip in the preview window and the timeline beneath.

Depending on your clip, you can choose to trim in three different ways:

*   Trim - If you only want to trim the start and end of your clip, select **Trim**.

- Click ▶ to start playing the clip. Set the In and Out points of the clip by clicking ⌈ and ⌉ , or by pressing the keys I and O. You can adjust the trim start and end points by dragging the in and out trim handles.

- Multi-trim - Select Multi-trim to split your clips into sections.

  Click ▶ to start playing the clip. Set the In and Out points of the clip by clicking ⌈ and ⌉ , or by pressing the keys I and O. You can adjust the trim start and end points by dragging the in and out trim handles.

  Click ✂ (or press **S**) to split your clip into separate sections. Each clip section is displayed at the right side of the dialog.

- Scene Detection - Select this option to let MoviePlus detect the scenes for you. It's most useful for very long clips that have been imported from either miniDV tapes or older video media.

  For more details on using the Trim dialog, see MoviePlus Help.

2. When you're happy with your clip(s) click **OK**. You're trimmed clip(s) are added to the **Media** pane **Project** tab.

To set the In (Start) and Out (End) points of a clip on the Timeline:

1. Add your video clip to the Video Track, then zoom into the timeline using the ⊕ **Zoom In** button.

   As you zoom in, more thumbnails appear representing the different frames in the clip. (The small marker above the thumbnail shows the exact time the frame will display in the **Video Preview** pane.)

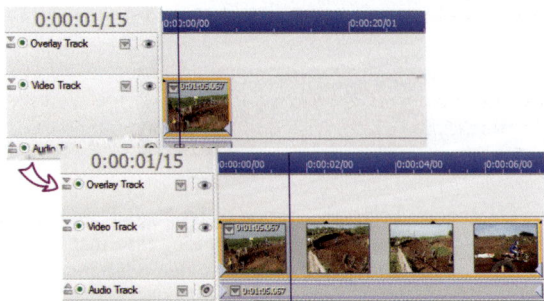

2.   Ensure the clip is selected.

3.   Click on the timeline ruler and drag the time indicator to where you want your clip to start. You can nudge the time indicator left or right by using the keyboard arrow keys.

The **Video Preview** pane will display the frame at this point.

(If you need to be more precise, zoom into the timeline further.)

4.   Press the **I** key to set the In point (or click **Select Start Time** from the right-click menu). The start of the clip is trimmed to the time indicator position.

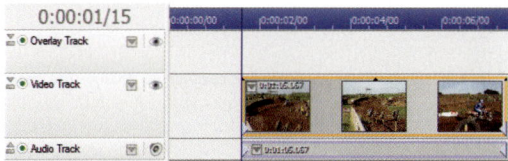

5.   Because the clip's duration is shorter, it also takes up less space on the timeline. If you have **Rippling** turned on, the clip will adjust itself on the timeline. Otherwise, click and drag the clip to the left to fill in the gap left on the timeline.

6.   Next, drag the time indicator to the frame where you want your clip to end. Press the **O** key (or click **Set End Time** from the right-click menu).

Notice that the audio track is trimmed at the same time. This is because the tracks are **linked**. (For more information on linking and unlinking clips, see MoviePlus Help.)

7.   Preview your clip to view the results. (You might need to press to 'rewind' the movie first.)

Trimming a clip does not delete any part of the clip itself; instead you can think of it as being hidden. This means that you can revise the trimming— either trim more to make the clip shorter or extend the clip to include more frames—without having to start the process from the beginning each time.

Linking and Rippling

If you have other clips on the timeline, you may need to move them to fill in the gaps that trimming creates:

• If your clips are linked, moving one clip will also move the linked clip.

• You can move linked and unlinked clips (and their associated relationships) at the same time with **Rippling**.

Click **Rippling** on the Timeline context toolbar to change the settings.

For details, see MoviePlus Help.

To use the trim cursor to modify a clip:

1. Click ⊕ **Zoom In** to increase the number of thumbnails displayed on the timeline. This will make it easier for you to be more accurate with your editing. (At the closest zoom, each frame will have its own thumbnail!)

2. Move the cursor over the clip's edge. When the cursor changes to the ⊕ **Trim** cursor, click and drag while keeping an eye on the **Video Preview** pane.

    You can either drag to make the clip smaller and remove frames, or you can drag in the opposite direction to add frames that were previously trimmed away.

3. Preview your movie to view the results.

> If you use the time indicator to mark the position of the frame, notice that the edge of the clip snaps to it as the cursor gets near. This handy editing feature is called **snapping**.

Splitting

There will be times where you will want to do something to the frames that are in the middle of a long clip. Perhaps you want to edit out frames that don't work well or remove that shot of the floor! You might also want to create more drama by adding a freeze-frame pause, or slow motion play, before continuing with the action. This can be achieved by splitting the clip.

Splitting turns one clip into two separate clips, without losing any frames in the process. The clips can then be trimmed or edited separately to achieve the effect that you want.

To split a clip:

1. Add your video clip to the Video Track, then zoom into the timeline using the ⊕ **Zoom In** button.

2. Click on the Timeline ruler and drag the time indicator to the point where you want to split your clip.

The **Video Preview** pane will display the frame at this point.

3.   Click to select your clip and then click the ✂ **Split** button on the Timeline context toolbar.

There are now two distinct clips on the timeline, but if you preview your movie, there will be no visible change.

4.   You can now edit the new clips individually.

When you split a clip, the linked audio track is also split at the same point.

Resizing Your Video

At some point in time, you'll want to resize your video, either to change the aspect ratio from normal (4:3) to widescreen (16:9) or to create some funky picture-in-picture or other animation effects. You'll be pleased to know that this is really easy to do in MoviePlus X5.

By the end of this tutorial you will be able to:

- Change the aspect ratio of a video clip.

- Change the size of a video clip using a transform.

- Change the size and perspective of a graphic.

- Use a preset transform.

Let's begin...

- Start a new DVD (Widescreen) or HD project, and import your movie clip to the **Media** pane **Project** tab.

Changing the aspect ratio

Many of us want to display our video on a widescreen TV, however, many camcorders are still in a native 4:3 format. Instead of accepting that you'll have to watch it with black lines either side, why not change the aspect ratio to 16:9?

> This tutorial shows you how to convert 'old style' 4:3 media to widescreen 16:9 format. If you have a camcorder that uses a widescreen (or HD) format by default, you could always substitute a video clip with a standard photo, or use one of the overlay samples in the **Media** pane **Library** tab to try out this example.

To change the aspect ratio from 4:3 to 16:9:

1. Drag the clip (or image/overlay) onto the timeline (or storyboard). When prompted to update the project settings to match the media, click **No**.

    The clip will display in the **Preview** window.

2. With the clip selected, on the context toolbar, click ⬜ **Fit**. In the drop-down list, click **Crop**.

    The clip is expanded to fit the new aspect ratio and the top and bottom part of the clip is cropped.

Hopefully, when you were filming your clip, you ensured that your subject had plenty of headroom. If not, you might end up cropping the subject as in the following examples.

The best thing about cropping a clip in MoviePlus is that it's very easy to reposition the crop for maximum effect.

To modify a crop:

1. On the timeline, the clip has a Grey/Yellow attributes button to show that one or more of the attributes has been modified.

Click the button to reveal the attributes menu and click **Crop**.
Notice that a single keyframe is displayed in the Crop envelope and is red to show it's selected.

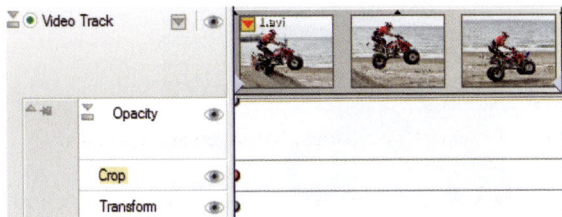

2.   Click to expand the **Properties** pane.

The selected (and only) keyframe is displayed as a thumbnail.

3.   Drag the time indicator to the position where the crop needs to be changed. On the Crop strip, hover the cursor over the time indicator and when the cursor changes to + click once to insert a keyframe.

4. On the **Properties** pane, the new keyframe is displayed in the thumbnail. Drag the crop up or down as appropriate.

5. Continue to add keyframes and position the crop as necessary. The number of keyframes that you'll need to use depends entirely on you video clip.

6. Play back your clip and view the results!

Keyframes

If you are modifying an existing keyframe, remember to select it first!

If you make a mistake and want to remove a keyframe, click to select it and then press the **Delete** key.

To delete all of the keyframes at once, click on the strip header and press the **Delete** key. **Warning**: this will remove **all** the keyframes on the clip.

You can also crop a video to remove unwanted distortion at the edges of your clips.

To change crop size:

1. On the timeline, ensure that the crop attributes are displayed and select the keyframe that you want to modify.

2. In the **Properties** pane, drag on the crop handles to resize the crop. (If **Match project aspect** in selected, the aspect ratio will be maintained.)

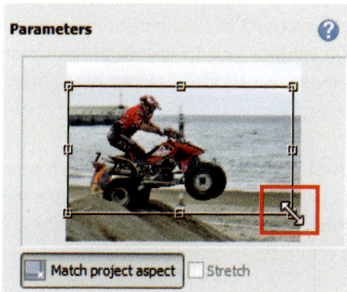

Pan and zoom

The **Crop** envelope is also used to pan and zoom your video clip. You'll find a lot of useful presets in the **Crop** envelopes found in the **Gallery** pane **Envelopes** tab.

Changing the size, rotation and position of your clip

There will be times when you'll want to change the size, rotation, perspective or position of your video clip or graphic overlay. This is done using the **Transform** envelope. When used in conjunction with multiple keyframes, the Transform envelope enables you to create great looking Picture-in-Picture and animation effects. It can also help to 'straighten' wayward footage.

The Transform envelope can be used on an individual clip, a keyframe, or it can be applied at track level (or a combination). The principles are the same whether using a CG clip (QuickShape or Text), still image or a video clip.

To add a preset transform to a clip:

1. Open a new project in timeline mode and then click **Insert > CG clip > QuickShape**.

2. In the **Properties** pane, on the **Properties** tab, change the **QuickShape type** to **Arrow** using the drop-down menu.

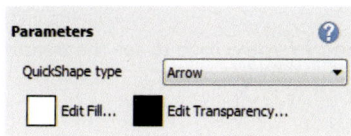

3. Click the **Galleries** pane and then click to display the **Envelopes** tab.

4. Click ⊞ to expand the **Transform** folder, and then the **Scroll** folder.

    The thumbnails show a preview of the effect. Some previews are animated. Hover over these to get a 'live' preview of the effect.

5. To add the effect to your clip, drag the thumbnail from the Galleries pane and drop it on top of your clip.

6. Preview your clip in the **Video Preview** pane to see the transform in action.

To reset the transform:

• To reset the clip, right-click the Transform strip header and select **Reset to Default**.
   - or -

• Select the Transform strip header and in the **Properties** pane, click **Reset**.

⚠ This will remove all but the first keyframe on the strip.

To rotate a clip using a preset transform:

1. Click the **Galleries** pane and then click to display the **Envelopes** tab.

2. Click ⊞ to expand the **Transform** folder, and then the **Rotate** folder.

3. Drag one of the rotate thumbnails from the **Galleries** pane and drop it on top of your clip. The clip is rotated.

To rotate a clip in the Video Preview pane:

1. On the timeline, on the QuickShape I clip, click the ▼ **Attributes** button and choose **Transform** from the drop-down menu.

2. Hover the cursor next to one of the bounding box handles. When it changes to the rotate cursor (highlighted), click and drag to rotate the clip.

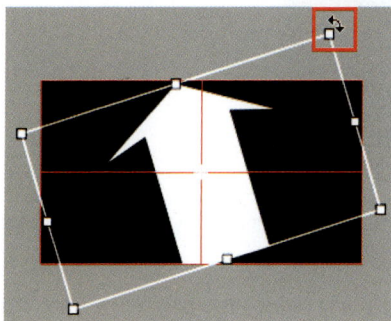

3. In the **Properties** pane, click **Reset** to undo all of your changes.

To change the size of a clip in the Video Preview pane:

1. On the timeline, on the QuickShape I clip, click the ▼ **Attributes** button and choose **Transform** from the drop-down menu.

2. In the **Video Preview** pane, click and drag on one of the bounding box handles to change the shape and size of the clip.

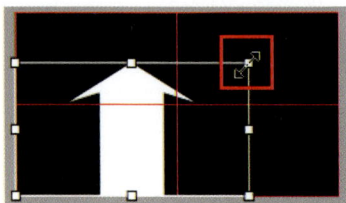

   (If you press the **Shift** key while dragging, you can change the aspect ratio of the clip.)

   Try dragging the clip so that it is bigger than the preview window (you may need to zoom out using **Zoom Out** on the **Video Preview** pane so that you can see the clip's bounding box).

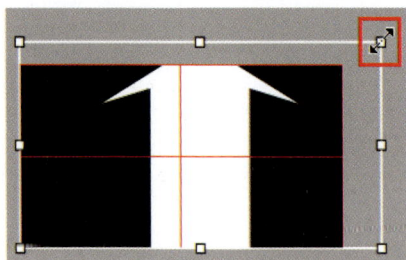

3. In the **Properties** pane, click **Reset** to undo all of your changes.

To change the size and rotation of a clip using the Properties pane:

1. On the timeline, on the QuickShape I clip, click the ▾ **Attributes** button and choose **Transform** from the drop-down menu.

2. In the **Properties** pane, in the **Parameters** section of the **Properties** tab, change the **X scale** and **Y scale** percentage values to 200%. Your clip is now twice its original size.

3. Change the **X scale** and **Y scale** percentage values to 50% to make your clip half of its original size.

4. Change the **Rotation (degrees)** value to 45. The clip is rotated 45 degrees to the left.

5. Change the **Rotation (degrees)** value to -45 to rotate the clip 45 degrees to the right.

6. Click **Reset** to undo all of your changes.

To change the perspective of a clip:

1. On the timeline, on the QuickShape I clip, click the ▾ Attributes button and choose **Transform** from the drop-down menu.

2. On the **Video Preview** pane, press the **Ctrl** key and click and drag on one of the bounding box handles.

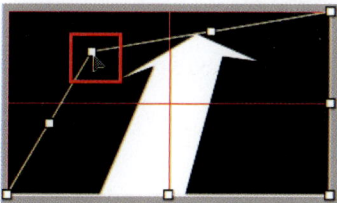

3. Experiment by **Ctrl**-dragging the other handles in various directions.

4. In the **Properties** pane, click **Reset** to undo all of your changes.

You can use transforms to create split screen effects, Picture in Picture (PiP), fade your movie into the distance as it ends, or even straighten that lopsided horizon on your favourite home movie!

When combined with other editing techniques (and a little bit of imagination), the possibilities are endless!

If you create a transform that you really like you can save it for later use:

1. On the timeline, select the transform envelope that you want to save.

2. In the **Properties** pane, click **Add to Gallery**.

3. Type a new name for your transform and click **OK**.

The custom transform envelope will now be listed with the other presets in the **Galleries** pane.

Video Overlays

Overlays have a range of applications in movie editing. They can be used to create decorative surrounds, watermarks and signatures, and to display information, especially for sporting events. Graphic overlays can also add interest to slide shows and enhance other video techniques. The MoviePlus timeline allows you to create an unlimited number of tracks. This means that you have the ability to overlay multiple 'layers' of clips, text and graphics.

By the end of this tutorial you will be able to:

• Add a preset overlay to a clip.

• Create a watermark using text objects.

Let's begin...

• Open a new project in timeline mode and then import a video clip to the **Media** pane **Project** tab.

Types of overlay

As a general rule, overlays in movie editing allow part of the underlying track to be visible. This means that they must have transparent sections, reduced opacity or be much smaller in size than the underlying clip. Overlays essentially fall into two categories—text based or graphical (the graphic overlay can be an image or video clip).

> This tutorial assumes that you know how to add media and tracks to your timeline. If you are unsure about how to do this, see the MoviePlus Help.

Graphic overlays

Graphic overlays are usually images or animations with transparent sections that allow the video clip beneath to show through. You'll find a variety of preset overlays for you to use in your projects in the **Media** pane, in the **Library** tab's **Samples** folder.

To add a graphic overlay:

1. Add your video and/or image clips to the Video Track.

By default a new project contains four tracks: 'Overlay Track' for titles, caption and other overlays and 'Video Track' for clips (illustrated above), plus two audio tracks, 'Audio Track' for the clip audio and 'Music Track' for additional background audio (not shown).

2. Drag the **ht223.mov** thumbnail to your Overlay Track.

3. Depending on your project settings, the overlay may not completely fit the clip.

If this is the case, to resize the overlay, experiment with the **Fit** options on the Context toolbar. (In this example, we used **Stretch** from the drop-down list.)

> The duration of an overlay clip can be altered in the same way as any other clip of that type. You can trim or extend the clip and/or add a transition in and out. If you are unsure how to do this see MoviePlus Help.

4. Preview your movie to see the overlay in action.

Watermarks or 'video bugs'

A watermark (or video bug) is text or a small logo that is displayed during part or all of the movie. Watermarks are commonly used by television broadcasters to display the name of the channel, but they can also be used to add the company name, date of creation, advertise website URLs, or as a personal signature by the movie creator.

To create a watermark:

1. Select the Overlay Track and ensure that it is empty by deleting any previous overlay. Drag the time indicator to the beginning of the track and click **T. Add Text** to add a new text clip.

2. In the **Video Preview** pane type in the text that you want to use for your watermark—we used 'mXtv' for 'Motocross TV'—then, click in the **Video Preview** pane, away from the text to deselect it. You'll see a bounding box around the text object.

3. In the **Properties** pane, click the **Format** tab and choose a suitable font from the drop-down list, or choose a bold preset with drop-shadow as we've done here.

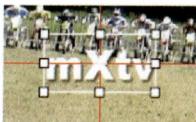

4. In the **Video Preview** pane:

    • Drag the handles of the bounding box to change the size and shape of your text.

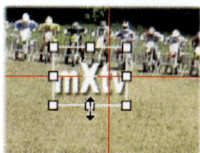

- Rotate the object by hovering your mouse pointer next to one of the corner handles, and then clicking and dragging the bounding box.

- Reposition the text object by dragging it to the desired location.

5. In the **Properties** pane, click the **Properties** tab. Change the text **Opacity** to 40%.

   This makes your watermark look a lot more subtle.

6. With your text clip still selected, on the timeline, drag the clip's
border so that it extends to the end of the movie.

7. Preview the movie to see your watermark in place.

Combining overlays

You can combine overlays to achieve various effects. When working with
multiple tracks and overlays, the order in which they are stacked is critical.
Usually your main footage is at (or near) the bottom of the stack; a
watermark should be placed at the top of the stack. All other overlay
tracks will lie somewhere in between the two.

You can create your own graphical overlays by using image editing software
such as Serif PhotoPlus. All you need to do is create an image that has some
transparent areas and save it to a 24 or 32-bit PNG format (with
transparency). You can then add it to your MoviePlus project via the **Import
Media** button on the **Media** pane.

Freeze-Frame and Looping

At some point you're bound to want to freeze the action, or even loop a sequence, to create some dramatic effects during your movies. Freeze-frames are also a great way to add a background to credit and title text. This is quick and easy to do with MoviePlus and we'll show you how in the next few pages.

By the end of this tutorial you will be able to:

- Extend a video clip using freeze-frames.

- Loop an audio/video clip.

Let's begin...

- Open a new project in timeline mode and then import a video clip to the **Media** pane **Project** tab.

Extending clips with 'freeze-frame'

Freeze-frames can be used as a background to title or credit text at the start or end of a movie, during a zoom to give the subject emphasis, or to give time for transitions between scenes.

You may also need to use freeze-frames to achieve some special editing effects—to allow you to freeze the action while overlaying a CG special effect, or to make time for drama-intensifying narration, for example.

To add a freeze-frame to the end of a clip:

1. Add your video clip to the Video Track and if necessary, use the scroll bar to scroll to the end of the clip.

2. With the clip still selected, in the **Properties** pane, on the **Properties** tab, select the **Enable Clip Extending** check box and the **Static** option.

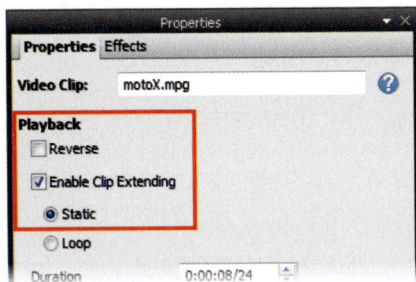

3. On the timeline, hover over the edge of the clip.

    When you see the **Extend clip** cursor, click and drag the edge of the clip to the right.

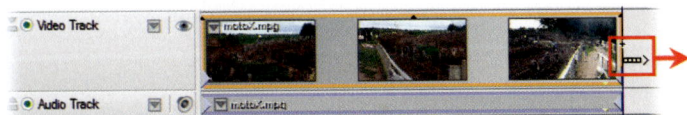

This extends the clip by freezing the final frame for the duration that you set by the drag operation.

4.   Preview your clip in the **Video Preview** pane to see the effect in action. (Click to 'rewind' the movie to the start.)

As your clip is extended, you will see a small yellow marker (under the clip). This marker shows the original start or end point of your clip, before your static extension was applied.

The black markers along the top of the clip indicate the position of the thumbnail previews. As the clip grows or shrinks on the timeline, the thumbnails will change as they show different frames within the clip.

To add a freeze-frame to the start of a clip:

1.   On the timeline ruler, drag to set the time indicator to approximately two seconds.

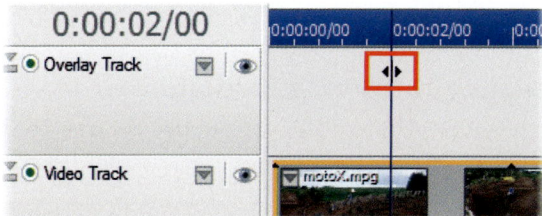

2. On the timeline, click and drag your clip to the right, so that the edge of the clip is in line with the time indicator.

3. In the **Properties** pane, on the **Properties** tab, select the **Enable Clip Extending** check box and select the **Static** option.

4. On the timeline, hover over the edge of the clip.
    When you see the **Extend clip** cursor, click and drag the edge of the clip to the left, so that it starts at 0:00:00/00.

    This freezes the first frame of the clip for a duration of two seconds.

5. Preview your clip from the start in the **Video Preview** pane to see the effect in action.

To add a freeze-frame to the "middle" of a scene:

This is a bit of a cheat as you actually have to split your clip into two where you want the freeze-frame to be. However, it's really easy to do.

1. On the timeline, ensure that the clip is selected and drag the time indicator to the point at which you want to add the freeze-frame. Click ✄ **Split** on the Context toolbar.

2. Click to select the left-hand clip again and on the Context toolbar, ensure that ⌘ ˙ **Rippling** is on.

3. In the **Properties** pane, select **Enable Clip Extending** with the **Static** option.

4. On the timeline, drag the right edge of the selected clip to the right, the other clip(s) will automatically move along the timeline so that the clip doesn't overlap.

When you preview your movie, it will appear as though the scene freezes and then restarts where it left off.

★ **Trimmed clips**

When you select the **Enable Clip Extending** option, trimming a clip on the timeline with the ⊞ **Trim** cursor is temporarily disabled. This allows you to extend trimmed clips rather than 'untrimming' them.

Looping clips

You can also extend a clip by looping—repeating a clip over a set amount of time. This is most effective when used with a clip that will loop seamlessly. The following example uses an animation style video clip; however, the technique is exactly the same for audio clips. Looping an audio clip is especially useful when you want a background track to play continues throughout your video or slideshow.

To loop a clip:

1. Open a new project in timeline mode and then in the **Media** pane, on the **Library** tab, click ⊞ to expand the **Samples** folder.

2. Next, expand the **Tutorials Workspace** folder and drag the **loop.mp4** thumbnail to the 'Video Track'.

3. With the clip still selected, in the **Properties** pane, on the **Properties** tab, select the **Enable Clip Extending** check box and select the **Loop** option.

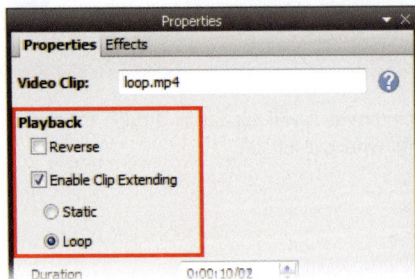

4.   On the timeline, hover over the edge of the clip.

When you see the ▥▸ **Extend clip** cursor, click and drag the edge of the clip to the right.

The clip will loop as it is extended on the timeline. The number of loops is shown by the yellow triangular markers displayed beneath the clip; each marker represents one full loop (there are three full loops in our example).

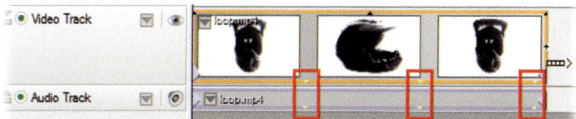

5.   Preview the results in the **Video Preview** pane.

Looping different file formats

Seamless looping is not possible with WMA and MP3 audio files as these are not 'gapless' formats—there is always a few milliseconds of blank audio at the end of the file. However, you can always trim the blank audio away in the Trim dialog to create a seamless loop.

WAV files are completely 'gapless' and will loop seamlessly without trimming.

Now that you know how to apply clip extending, there's so much more you can do. Why not try adding a text clip to the Overlay track so that you can use your freeze-frame image as a background to the movie title or to add interest to the credits?

Have fun!

Slow Motion Effect

There are times when you'll want to create a slow-motion effect for your video, and it's especially useful for that all-important action replay! The best thing about creating this effect is that it's really easy to do in MoviePlus. We'll show you how in this short tutorial.

By the end of this tutorial you will be able to:

* Change the playback speed of a clip to create a slow-motion effect.

Let's begin...

* Open a new project in timeline mode and then import a video clip to the **Media** pane **Project** tab.

Changing the playback speed

Creating that slow-motion replay is really as simple as changing the speed that the clip plays at. Of course, if you don't want to effect the entire clip, you'll need to split the clip into relevant sections first (see *Trimming & Splitting* on p. 83).

🖈 In our examples, we only show a single 2 second clip on the timeline for ease of reference. Obviously, your timeline may contain many more clips and tracks.

To create a slow motion effect:

1. Add a short (trimmed) video clip to the Video Track, then zoom into the timeline using the ⊕ **Zoom In** button.

2. With the clip selected, expand the **Properties** pane, **Properties** tab. By default, the **Play speed** is **1.000**.

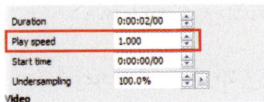

Duration	0:00:02/00	⬍
Play speed	1.000	⬍
Start time	0:00:00/00	⬍
Undersampling	100.0%	⬍ ▸
Video		

3. Click the down arrow to reduce the speed to 0.800. The clip **Duration** increases (it takes longer to play the clip), and this is also shown on the timeline as the clip takes up more space.

Duration	0:00:02/13	⬍
Play speed	0.800	⬍
Start time	0:00:00/00	⬍
Undersampling	100.0%	⬍ ▸

At half speed (0.500) the clip will take twice as long to play.

4. Preview your clip to see the results.

To change playback speed on the timeline:

1.   On the timeline, click to select the clip.

2.   Press and hold the **Ctrl** key and drag the right edge of the clip to the
     right with the ⇥⤳ cursor to make the clip longer.

     Preview the clip. You'll notice that the action is even slower.

3.   Press and hold the **Ctrl** key and drag the right edge of the clip to the
     left with the ⇥⤳ cursor to make the clip shorter.

     Preview the clip. You'll notice that the action is much quicker again.

That's it!

Split Screen Effect

As its name suggests, the split screen is a technique in which two or more movie or image clips are displayed simultaneously on different parts of the screen.

This effect is popular in many TV shows and sports channels and can be used as a way of adding drama or to display action simultaneously. For example, you could show both sides of a telephone call; show the action from the sports race leaders or compare time splits in a race; or use it as a way of leading into another related video clip.

By the end of this tutorial you will be able to:

• Create a split screen effect using preset transforms.

Let's begin...

• Open a new project in timeline mode and then import a video clip to the **Media** pane **Project** tab.

To create a split screen effect, you will need to use multiple video tracks as each "split" will need its own track. Although for this example you can use the same clip over and over, ideally, you'll need at least four different clips (or images).

Using presets to divide the screen

The next few steps will introduce you to the split screen by applying a
transform to a single keyframe at a track level. However, the same
techniques can also be applied to clips, and over multiple keyframes to
achieve some spectacular effects.

To create a 4-way split screen effect:

1. Press **F9** (or click **Insert > Video track**) and insert three more
    tracks so that you have four in total.

    Resize the timeline by dragging the top edge so that you can see all of
    the tracks at the same time.

2. Drag a clip to each of the video tracks.

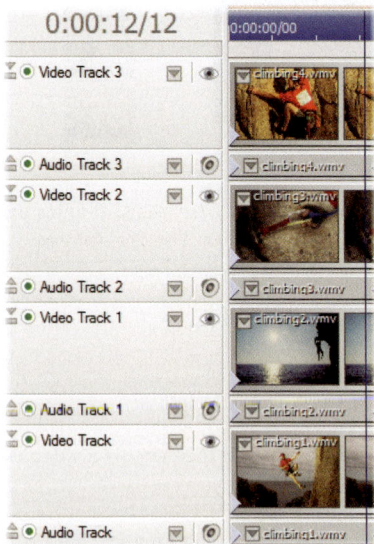

Don't worry that you can't see all of your clips in the **Video
Preview** pane, we'll come to that in a minute.

Each clip needs to be changed in size and position. We could do this manually for each clip—sometimes this can create a great custom effect. However, let's make MoviePlus do the hard work for us and use one of the preset transforms.

3.   Expand the **Galleries** pane and click the **Envelopes** tab.

4.   Navigate to and expand the **Transform** folder. Next expand the **Split Screen** and **Quad** folders.

5.   Drag the **Quad Bottom Left** thumbnail from the **Galleries** pane and drop it onto the 'Video Track 3' header. The clip updates.

6. Next, add a different 'Quad' transform—**Quad Top-Right**, **Quad Bottom-Right** and **Quad Bottom-Left**—to each remaining video track.

7. Preview your movie from the start. You should see all of your clips playing simultaneously.

Finishing touches

To complete the effect, there are a few more things you could do, for example:

• Add background music or mute all other audio apart from one track.

• Add title text (use a QuickShape if necessary to emphasise the text).

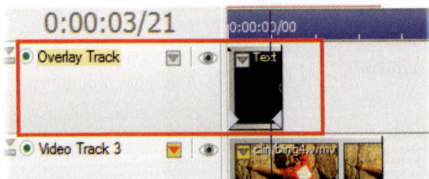

• Apply a crop to each movie or image clip using to refine the look and remove any black borders. (Or even modify each clip's transform envelope to add black borders!

The split screen effect essentially includes any instance when the screen is divided into more than one picture, including **Picture in Picture**. As this is such a popular effect, we've dealt with it in a separate tutorial. See *Picture in Picture* on p. 131 for more information.

Some types of split screen work best when used in conjunction with masks and video groups. See the section *Advanced Masking* on p. 147 in the *Masks* tutorial for more information.

Shortcut keys are available for many of the common tasks. For example, the **F9** key adds a new video track. The shortcut key is either displayed in the menu next to the command or on the tooltip (if a button).

Picture in Picture (PiP)

The Picture in Picture (PiP) technique can be used to add fun effects to your movies or slideshows. For example, PiP can be used to display different camera angles simultaneously or show close ups of the star sportsman as well as the entire game. PiP has its uses for tutorial style videos too!

In this tutorial, you'll learn how to:

• Create a simple PiP effect using only two video tracks.

• Adjust PiP audio.

The Picture in Picture effect looks really impressive and can create an element of fun. Although it can take on many forms, the techniques used to create the PiP in MoviePlus are very similar.

Let's begin...

• Open a new project in timeline mode and then import a video clip to the **Media** pane **Project** tab.

Creating a simple Picture in Picture effect

To create Picture in Picture, you will need to use at least two video tracks. Ideally, you'll need at least two different clips (or images). The effect we are about to create is one commonly used in tuition videos (e.g., martial arts, guitar tuition) so that the viewer can see more than one angle at the same time.

To create a simple PiP effect:

1. Add your main video clip (or image) to the Video Track. This will be the primary, full-size clip.

    If necessary, change the ⬜ **Fit** to match your project settings. (See *Resizing your video* on p. 91 if you're unsure how to do this.)

2. Click the track header and then, in the **Properties** pane, on the **Properties** tab, rename the track 'Primary Video'.

3. Click the 'Primary Video' track header and then click **Insert > Video Track**. Check that this track is **above** the 'Primary Video' track. If not, use the **Arrange** menu to reorder the tracks.

4.   Drag your PiP video clip from the **Media** pane to the 'Video Track 1', leaving a second or two gap before the clip starts.

The grid-like box indicates that a new audio track will be created on release.

If you preview your movie in the **Video Preview** pane, you will see that the second video clip starts 5 seconds into your movie, but it obscures the background video clip.

Let's change the size of the second clip to create the PiP effect.

The size of the clip is changed by using a **transform**. We will need to apply this at track level so that it effects the entire PiP track.

5. Expand the **Galleries** pane and click the **Envelopes** tab.

6. Navigate to and expand the **Transform** folder. Next expand the **Split Screen** and **Quad** folders.

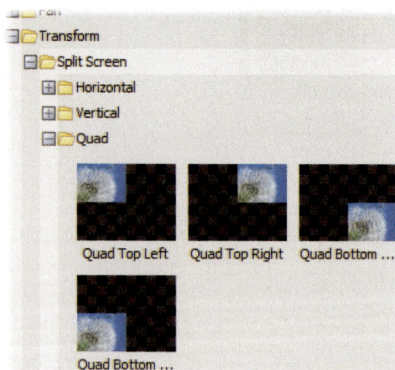

7. Drag the **Quad Bottom Left** thumbnail from the **Galleries** pane and drop it onto the 'Video Track 1' header.

8. In the **Video Preview** pane, resize and reposition the clip if necessary.

9. Preview your movie to see the effect. (You might need to press to 'rewind' the movie first.)

Why not add some title text to your movie? Select the 'Overlay Track' and either insert a **Text clip** from the **Insert > CG clip** menu or use a title preset from the **Galleries** pane **Titles** tab.

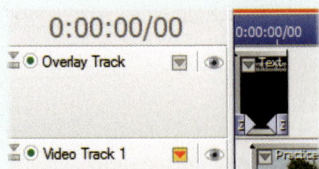

PiP audio

If you have used two video clips, you may notice that the audio plays for both clips at the same time. There are several ways that you can approach this:

- Mute only the unwanted audio track.

  - or -

- Apply a volume envelope to the audio clips (or tracks) so that you can 'blend' the clips together.

  - or -

- Mute all of the original audio track(s) and insert background music or narration.

See the *Audio Techniques* tutorial on p. 155 for more information about managing audio clips.

Using these techniques, you can create some really impressive Picture in Picture effects. This effect can also be used at any point in a movie—just move the clips to a different point on the timeline.

Above all, have fun experimenting!

💡 **Learn shortcuts!**

Shortcut keys are available for many of the common tasks. For example, the **F9** key adds a new video track, **F11** adds a video group. The shortcut key is either displayed in the menu next to the command or on the tooltip on the button.

Masks

Masking is a technique that allows you to hide one part of your video while revealing another. Masks enable you to quickly create special effects, create space for credits and to creatively change the shape of the movie border.

By the end of this tutorial you will be able to:

- Add a simple mask to a track.

- Create a mask from a QuickShape.

- Use video groups to mask one clip and reveal another.

Let's begin...

- Open a new project in timeline mode and then import a video clip to the **Media** pane **Project** tab.

What are masks?

A mask is used to hide part of a movie or image clip, revealing an alternative clip or background. You can achieve many different effects using masks, for example, you can:

- 'Cut out' a video clip to give it an irregular shaped border or create interesting text.

- Hide part of a clip to make room for text and credits.

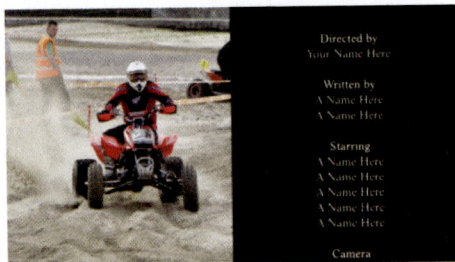

- Create special effects, split screen effects or a Picture in Picture by hiding part of a clip and revealing the clip on the track below.

Basic masks

The simplest masks are made up of a white area and a transparent area. When the track is set to a 'mask' blend mode, the white section reveals the clip on the tracks beneath the mask and everything else is hidden. Let's try this now.

In this example, we'll apply the mask to the entire length of the clip. However, in a 'real' movie, the effect will often only be applied to a small section of the movie, commonly the start or end. This is an ideal time to use a freeze-frame clip or even a selection of still images!

To add a mask to a clip:

1. Add your video clip to the Video Track.

We've selected a clip where the subject is to the left of the picture. This is because we're going to hide the right half of the screen to leave room for our credits.

2. Click **Insert > Video Track** and in the **Properties** pane, rename this new track 'Mask'.

3. In the **Media** pane, click the **Library** tab to display it. Click ⊞ to expand the **Samples** folder, the **Tutorials Workspace** folder and finally, the **Masks** folder. Drag the **LeftHalf.png** thumbnail onto the new 'Mask' track.

4. Hover the pointer over the right edge of the mask image clip and use the ⊹ trim cursor to extend it to the length of your video clip.

5. If necessary, with the clip still selected, click ▢ **Fit** and choose **Stretch** from the drop-down menu. The white rectangle is stretched to cover the left-half of the preview pane.

6. Click on the header of the 'Mask' track to select it. Then, in the **Properties** pane, in the **Video** section, change the **Blend Mode** to **Mask**.

7. In the **Video Preview** pane, the section of the video clip on the left of the screen has been revealed and the right side is now black—a perfect place to add credits!

In the next few steps, we'll show you how to add a title clip to your video. For more information about text clips, see MoviePlus Help.

To add credits and adjust the mask start time:

1. Expand the **Galleries** pane and select the **Titles** tab.

2. Click ⊞ to expand the **Presets** folder, and then the **Credits** folder. Drag the **Modern Center Aligned Credits** thumbnail to the 'Overlay Track'.

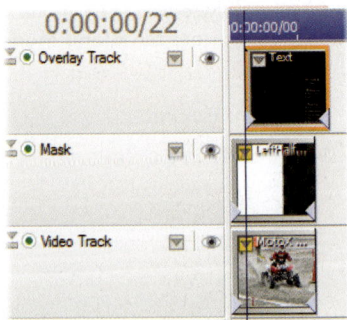

3. Hover the mouse pointer over the right edge of the text clip and use the ⊩ trim cursor to fit the clip to the end of the movie.

If you preview the movie, you'll see that the credits scroll right up the middle of the screen. Let's fix this now.

4. Drag the time indicator to a position on the timeline where you can clearly see the text. Then, click once on the text to display the text bounding box.

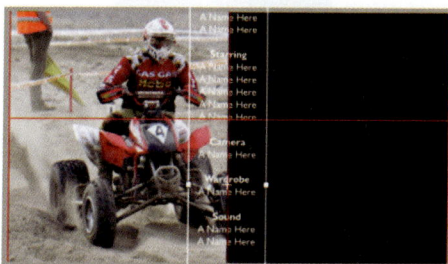

5. Drag the text into position in the centre of the black area.

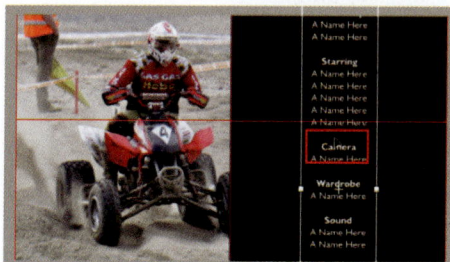

6. Preview your movie!

Now, all that's left to do is to change the point where the mask comes into effect.

To change the mask In and Out points:

1. If you need to, zoom into the timeline using the ⊕ **Zoom In** button.

2. Hover the mouse pointer over the left edge of the mask image clip and use the ⊞ trim cursor to drag the clip to the new start position, just before the start of the credit text.

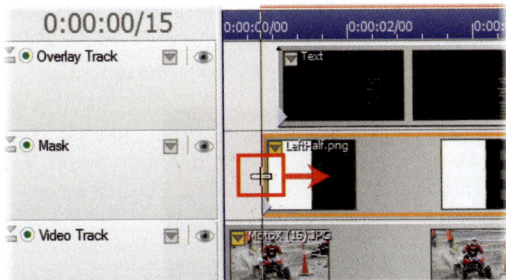

3. Finally, preview the effect in the **Video Preview** pane. (You might need to click 🔘 to 'rewind' the movie first.)

> ★ Notice that the movie plays at full screen size, then the mask appears, followed by your scrolling credit text. When a track is set to the Mask blend mode, it will only be applied to the underlying track when the mask track contains a clip. Where the track is empty, the underlying tracks will not be affected.

Advanced masking

So far, we have added a mask to tracks that are all on the same level on the timeline. This means that any clip that is on a track below the mask track will be affected. So, how do we create the effect where one clip plays alongside the other? If we just add another track beneath the mask track, both tracks will be affected by the mask. The answer is to use **video groups**. Let's try this now.

To use a mask to display two movie or image clips you need a video group and a minimum of three video tracks: two for movie or image clips, one for the mask.

To set up a video group for a mask:

1. Open a new project and add your media to the **Media** pane.

2. On the timeline, select the 'Video Track' and then press **F9** twice to add two new video tracks (alternatively, select **Insert Video Track** from the right-click menu). Select 'Video Track 2' and in the **Properties** pane, rename this new track 'Mask'.

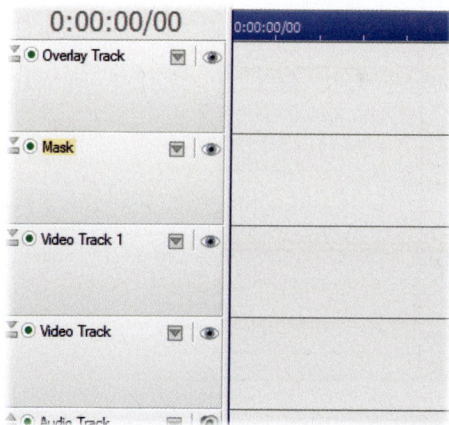

3. On the **Insert** menu, click **Video Group** (**F11**).

In the **Properties** pane, in the **Video Track** text box on the **Properties** tab, rename the group 'Mask group'.

4. Click the 'Mask' track header to select it and then, on the **Arrange** menu, click **Move Into Video Group**. Repeat for 'Video Track 1'.

Your timeline should look like the one illustrated.

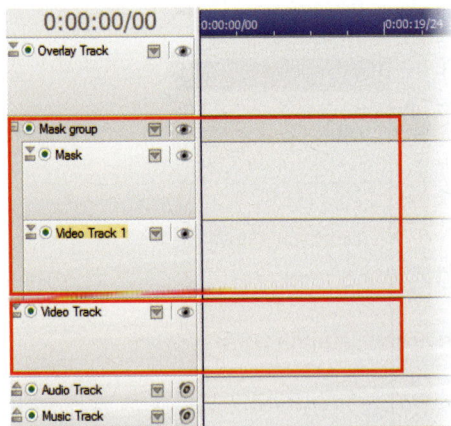

Key points:

- The 'Mask' track is above 'Video Track 1' and both are inside the group.

- The 'Video Track' is not in the group.

If necessary, rearrange the track order using the **Arrange** menu.

To use a mask within a video group

1. Drag your video (or image) clip onto the main 'Video Track' and **Fit** as necessary.

2. Drag your second video clip onto 'Video Track 2', so that it starts approximately 2 seconds after the main clip (and **Fit** as necessary).

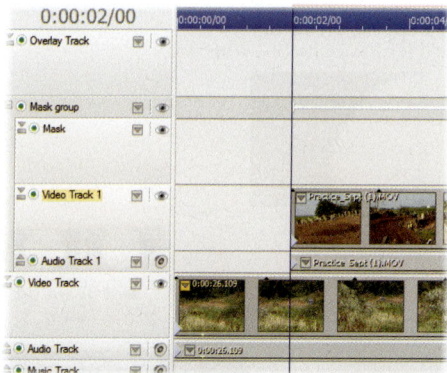

3. Expand the **Galleries** pane and click the **Envelopes** tab.

4. Navigate to and expand the **Transform** folder. Next expand the **Split Screen** and **Quad** folders.

5. Drag the **Quad Top Left** thumbnail from the **Galleries** pane and drop it onto the 'Video Track 1' header. The clip updates.

6. Click to select the 'Mask' track and position the time indicator at 2 seconds—in line with the start time of the 'Video Track 1' clip.

7. Click **Insert > CG clip > QuickShape**.

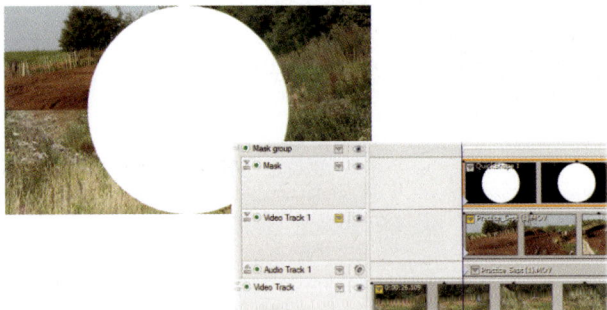

8. In the **Properties** pane, on the **Properties** tab, use the drop-down menu to change the **QuickShape type** to **Button**.

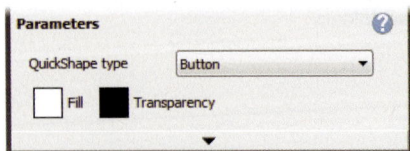

9. Drag the **Quad Top Left** thumbnail from the **Galleries** pane and drop it onto the 'Mask' header. The clip updates.

10. Optional: Drag the handles of the QuickShape so that the white shape sits just inside the second video clip.

11. On the timeline, drag the right edge of the QuickShape clip with the ⊕ trim cursor so that it matches the length of your 'Video Track 1' clip.

12. Click the 'Mask' track header to select the track, then, in the **Properties** pane, on the **Properties** tab, in the **Video** section, change the **Blend Mode** to **Mask**.

13. Preview your movie in the **Video Preview** pane to see the effect. (You might need to press to 'rewind' the movie first.)

The 'Movie 2' clip is now cut out into the shape of the QuickShape. This effect works with any QuickShape (or even an image clip) as long as it is coloured white.

Other mask examples

You can create masks from a variety of different images, and even from video clips. They work best with clips that have solid white areas and transparent sections. However, you can also create interesting effects by using coloured masks, text or even photos! Because the mask blend mode is set on the track, it means that the clip used as the mask can have keyframe animations, effects and transitions.

The following examples should give you some ideas. The techniques used are the same—they all have a track set to mask blend mode and use a video group to contain the mask—but the result is very different.

Example - Title mask

We added visual interest to our motocross opening title sequence by using the title text itself as a mask.

We added a second video track and renamed it 'Mask'. We then added a text clip to the 'Mask' track.

The text was formatted with a large, bold font and resized to fill the
Video Preview pane. We also added a CG background clip set to white
and overlapped it to create a long cross-fade to fade-out the mask while
the video is playing.

Finally, in the **Properties** pane, we set the blend mode on the track to
'**Mask**'.

The main video clip is played beneath the mask which fades out to show
the action!

Audio Techniques

To make a movie interesting, you're going to need some sort of soundtrack. Audio is 50% of the movie! This tutorial looks at how you can use multiple audio tracks to add special effects, narration and background sound.

By the end of this tutorial you will be able to:

•   Combine multiple audio tracks.

•   Insert and use timeline markers to precisely align clips.

•   Work with audio envelopes.

Let's begin...

•   Open a new project in timeline mode.

The importance of sound

Great movies all have one thing in common, a great soundtrack. Sound adds impact to a movie, and is in many ways more important than the video itself, even if you don't realise it at the time. A good background track, perhaps combined with narration, helps to add interest to slideshows and keep your audience's attention.

In this simple project, we'll create an opening sequence called "The Storm" by using a text clip and a few audio files to create the soundtrack. This will introduce you to the various audio techniques and effects that you can apply to your future projects.

To create the title clip:

1. On the timeline, click to select the 'Overlay Track' and on the **Video Preview** pane, click **T. Add Text**. A text clip in added to the 'Overlay Track'.

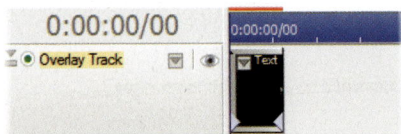

2. In the **Video Preview** pane, click inside the text box and type "The Storm". Change the font to something bold (we selected Impact) and large enough to fill most of the preview screen.

Next, we'll add a background to the text.

3. On the **Video Preview** pane, click **Add Image**. In the Add Image dialog, browse to a suitable image (any landscape type photo would be ideal) and click **Open**.

4. Place the image at the size you want by dragging the cursor. The image is placed on release.

5. To move the image behind the text, on the **Properties** pane, on the **Properties** tab, click **Move Back**.

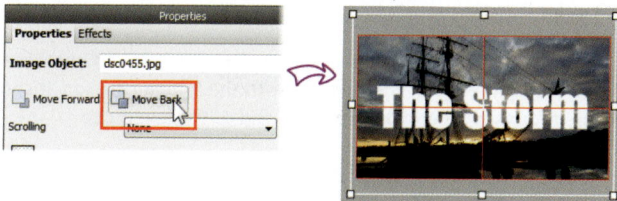

That's it for now, we'll come back to the title clip a little later on. For now, we'll move on to the audio.

To add an audio clip to the timeline:

1. Click to display the **Media** pane **Library** tab and then click ⊞ to expand the **Samples** folder, the **Tutorials Workspace** folder and finally the **Audio** folder.

2. Drag the **Rainshower.wma** clip to the 'Audio Track', ensuring that it starts at 0:00:00/00.

3. Zoom into the timeline using the ⊕ **Zoom In** button, so that the clip occupies a reasonable amount of the timeline. Next, click ⤓ to collapse the 'Video Track' as we won't need it.

4. You'll see that the audio clip is longer than our title. To correct this, drag the right edge of the title clip with the ⊩ trim cursor. It should snap into place when you reach the end of the audio clip.

5. If you preview the video from the beginning, you'll see the title and hear the accompanying rain shower.

⚠ **Don't forget to save your work!**

Adding additional audio clips

Although you can layer multiple audio clips on one audio track, it's easier to see what's going on when overlapping clips have their own track. (It also allows you to apply different effects to each clip.) Adding multiple audio tracks is virtually the same as adding extra video tracks, so these steps should feel really familiar.

To add additional audio tracks and add clips:

1. On the timeline, click to select the 'Audio Track' header and press the **F10** key. Alternatively, right-click and choose **Insert Audio Track** from the menu. A new audio track is inserted above 'Audio Track'.

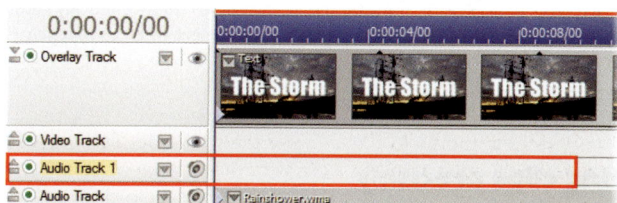

Repeat step 1 to add another audio track, so that you have three audio tracks in total.

Now, let's add some more audio clips!

2. Drag the time indicator to 0:00:01/00 on the timeline (you can use the arrow keys to nudge the time indicator into exact position).

3. Next, drag the **crowclose.wma** clip from the **Audio** folder onto 'Audio Track 1'. Notice how it snaps to the time indicator when it gets close to it (if not, you can turn on **Snapping** in the **Arrange** menu).

4. Preview the video from the beginning to listen to the new audio.

When you place clips on separate tracks, MoviePlus doesn't add any automatic transitions or cross-fades as you would otherwise get when overlapping clips on the same track.

Placing clips precisely

When you listen to the audio, you'll notice that there are two distinct bird calls, a gap, then two more. We want to place our next clip in the middle of the four calls. We could do this by trial and error, but there is a better way...

To view an audio waveform:

* On the Audio Track 1 header, click ▲ to restore the track to full
  height. The waveform is displayed on the timeline and you can clearly
  identify the four bird calls by the 'bumps' in the wave (silence is
  illustrated by a perfectly flat line).

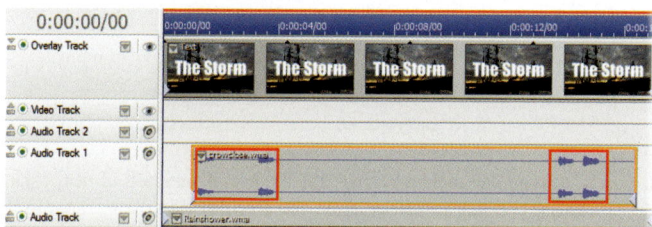

⚠ When editing HD clips or large audio files, it may be necessary to wait for a
short period of time for the waveform to be generated.

A storm isn't complete without thunder and this is going to be our final
audio clip. We're also going to add an extra special, 'lightning' effect to our
title, so to help us match the two events precisely, we can use a **timeline
marker**.

📌 Markers are visible even when tracks are minimized. This allows you to line up
clips or keyframes on multiple tracks.

To insert timeline markers:

1. On the timeline, drag the time indicator to position it at 0:00:08/00.

2. On the context toolbar, click 📍 and choose **Insert Marker** from
   the drop-down list (alternatively, press **F6**).

When you move the time indicator slightly, a green marker displays on the timeline.

3. The orange flag indicates that the Marker is selected (if not, click once on the green flag to select it). In the **Properties** pane, rename the marker "Thunder". (You can also finetune the position here as well.)

Now we can add our final effects.

Don't forget to save your work!

To align clips and effects:

1. Drag the **Thunder.wma** clip from the **Audio** folder onto 'Audio Track 2' and position it next to the new marker. This also snaps into place (if not, you can turn on **Snapping** in the **Arrange** menu).

2.   Preview the video from the beginning to listen to the new audio.

Next, we'll add matching 'lightning' to the text clip.

3.   Expand the **Galleries** pane and click the **Envelopes** tab. Click ⊞ to expand the **Opacity** folder and the **Flicker** folder, then drag the **2s Strong Flicker** thumbnail from the pane and drop it onto the text clip.

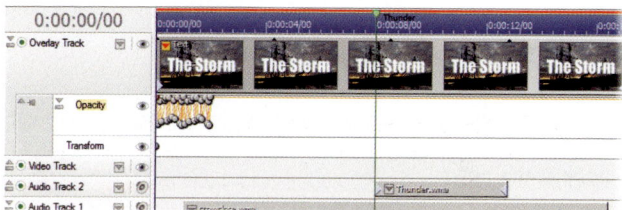

4.   Drag a selection box around the keyframes.

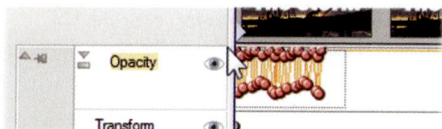

5.   On the **Edit** menu, click **Cut**, then on the timeline, drag the time indicator in-line with the 'Thunder' marker. Finally, on the **Edit** menu, click **Paste**.

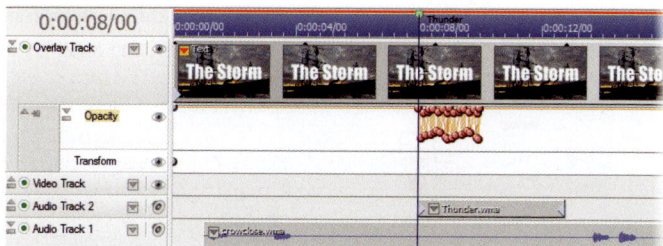

The keyframes are moved to the new location. Preview the video from the beginning to see and hear the completed effect!

> ⚠ When cutting and pasting keyframes, it's important that the envelope strip you are working on is selected. If the keyframes won't paste, click the envelope strip header and try again.

Audio effects and adjustments

There are times when you'll need to increase (or decrease) audio volume. You might also want to add a stereo pan or even some effects. Let's take a quick look at this now.

To change the volume on the track:

1. On the timeline, on the Audio Track 2 header, click the ▼ **Attributes** button and select **Volume** from the drop-down list. The envelope strip opens.

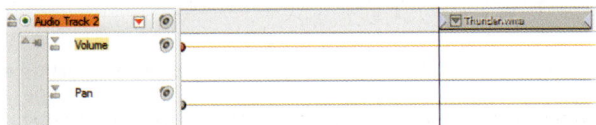

2. To change the volume on the entire track, drag the single keyframe down to reduce volume (illustrated) or up to increase volume.

3. To vary the volume you will need to use additional keyframes. Set the starting volume (first keyframe as in step 2) and then, drag the time indicator to the point where you want the next keyframe.

4. Click once on the strip to add a keyframe and then drag the keyframe up or down to achieve the desired volume at that position.

In the following example using three keyframes, the volume starts quiet, gets louder and then quieter again.

The shape of the line depends on the **Interpolation**, and can be changed in the **Properties** pane to create different effects (see MoviePlus Help for more information).

Interpolation

This is a mathematical calculation used to determine the rate of change (the shape of the line) between two keyframes.

You can use the volume envelope to fade (alternate) the audio between tracks. This is done by applying a volume envelope to each track. The keyframes are set at the same time, but at high volume on one envelope, and at low volume on the other.

When adding sound effects to your clips, it is often useful to mute the other audio tracks. You can turn mute on and off by clicking on the track header.

To pan audio from left to right:

1. On the timeline, click the **crowclose.wma** clip's ☑ **Attributes** button and select **Pan** from the drop-down list. The envelope strip opens.

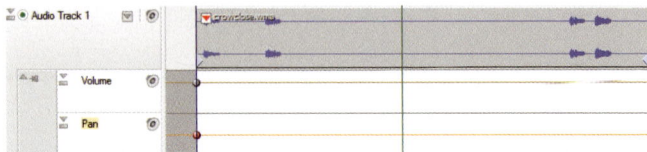

The first keyframe is positioned in the vertical centre of the strip. This shows that the audio is in the 'centre'—it plays at an equal volume through both speakers. (Preview the clip to try this for yourself).

2. Click to select the first keyframe and in the **Properties** pane, change the **Interpolation** to **Hold**.

3. On the timeline, drag the time indicator to the first space between the bird calls and click when the cursor changes to + to insert a keyframe. Drag this to the top of the envelope strip (i.e., 100% Left).

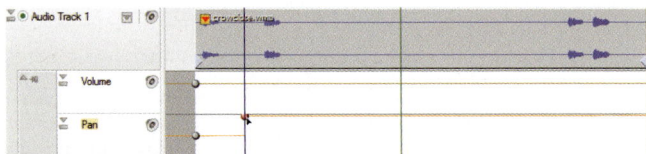

4. Insert another keyframe just before the next bird call and drag it all the way to the bottom, i.e., 100% Right (the interpolation will be remembered from the last time).

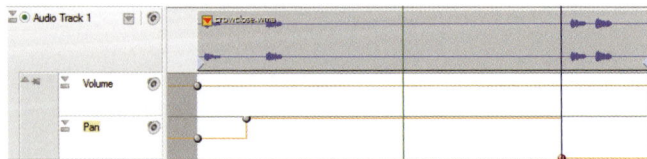

5. Finally, add a fourth keyframe just before the last bird call and drag it to the centre again (you can set this precisely in the **Properties** pane).

6. Preview the video from the beginning to listen to the effect.

You will notice that the crow sounds start in the centre, then come from the left speaker, then the right, and then in the centre again.

Experiment with the other audio tracks (or clips) and try more keyframes and different **interpolation** type to get the sound to pan gradually from one speaker to the other.

As you can see, there is so much you can do with audio, and we have only touched on the basics! The MoviePlus Help contains information about using **effects groups** to give you even more control over your audio effects.

As with any effect, some things you try will work, others won't. But you can still have a lot of fun finding out. Good luck!

3

Menu
Templates

Menu Templates

When you've finished editing your movie, open the Menu Designer and browse the wide selection of themed menu templates that are included with MoviePlus for use with your DVD, VCD, Blu-ray and AVCHD projects. All templates can be customized, so you're sure to find something to suit your needs.

The templates are categorized as follows:

- Animated
- Antique
- Celebrations
- Funky
- General
- Holiday and Festivities
- Home
- Kids and Baby
- Modern
- Moods
- Movie Styles
- Seasons
- Sports
- Wedding and Romance

💡 For details on customizing these templates, see the *How To pane* or *MoviePlus Help.*

Animated

Your Title
Chapter 1
Chapter 2
Chapter 3

Your Title
Chapter 1
Chapter 2
Chapter 3

Antique

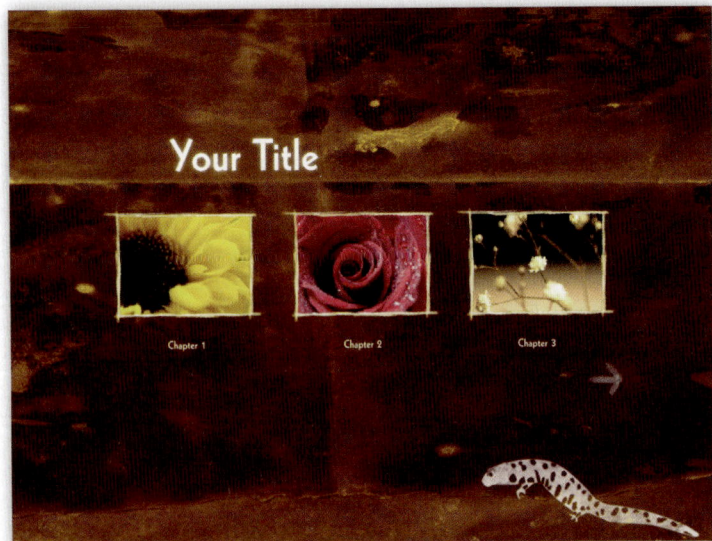

YOUR TITLE
CHAPTER 1
CHAPTER 2
CHAPTER 3
CHAPTER 4

Your Title
Chapter 1

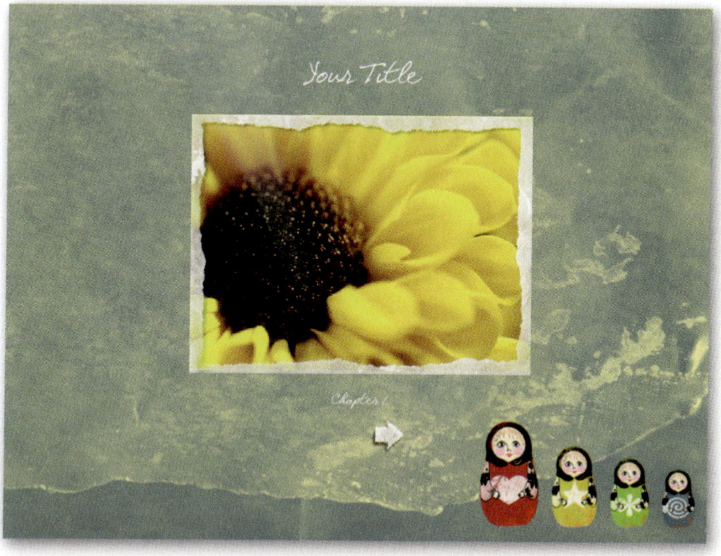
Your Title
Chapter 1

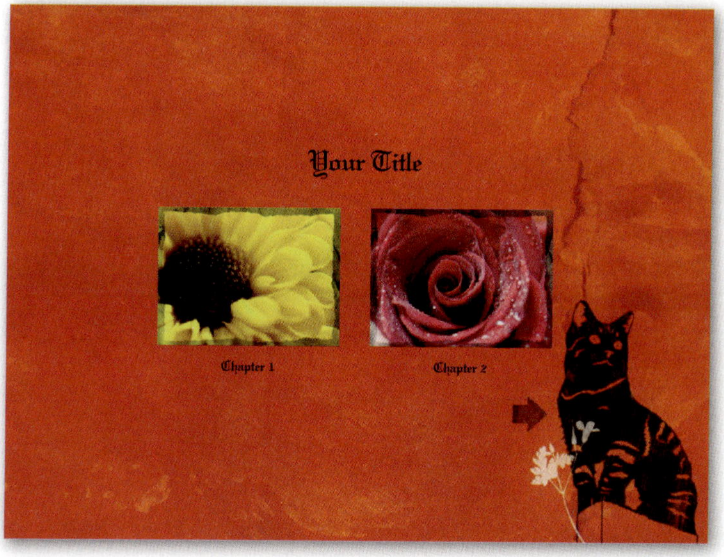
Your Title
Chapter 1
Chapter 2

Celebrations

Your Title
Chapter 1
Chapter 2

Your Title
Chapter 1
Chapter 2
Chapter 3
Chapter 4

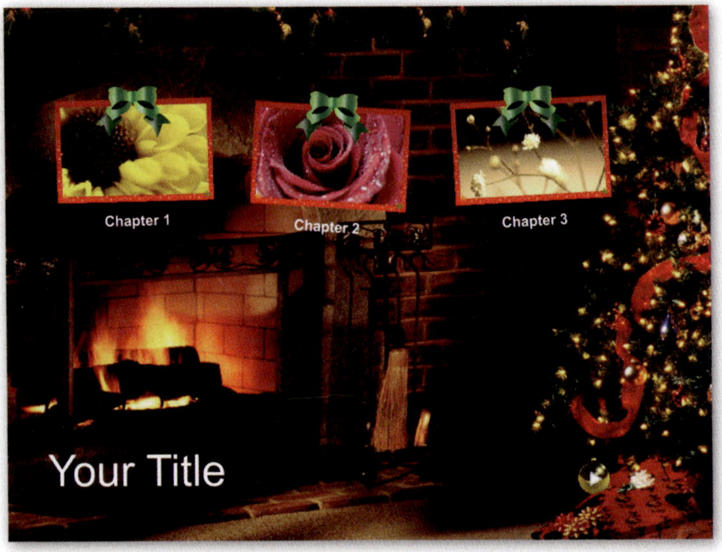
Chapter 1
Chapter 2
Chapter 3
Your Title

Funky

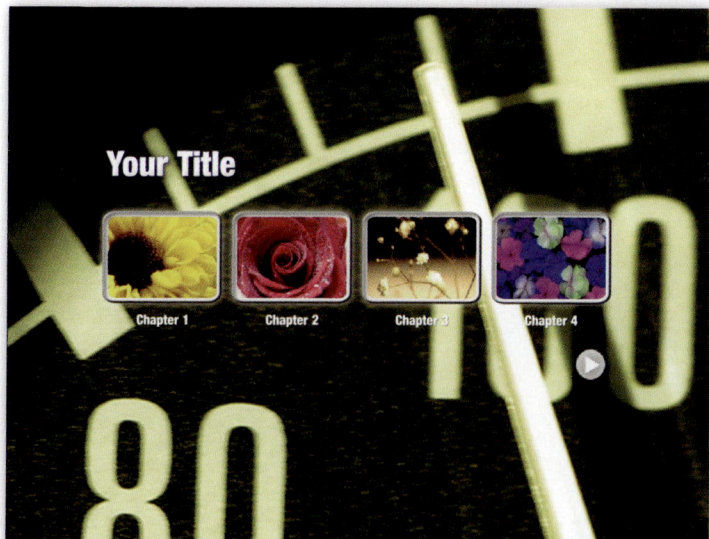

Your Title
Chapter 1
Chapter 2
Chapter 3
Chapter 4

Your Title
Chapter 1
Chapter 2
Chapter 3
Chapter 4

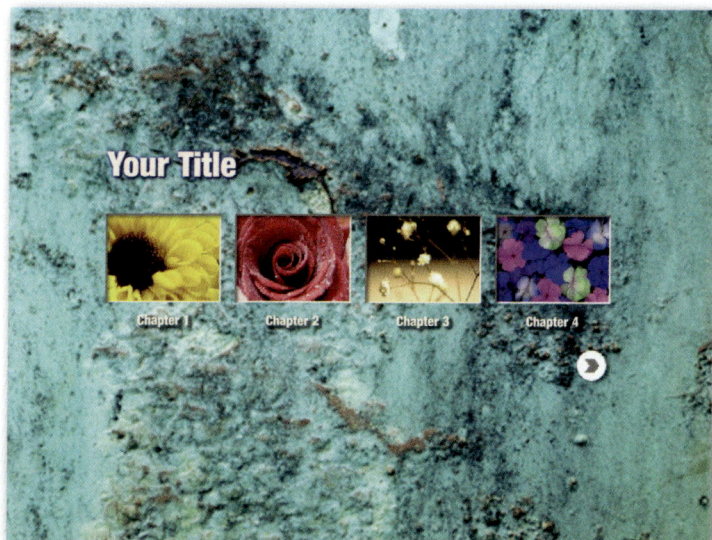

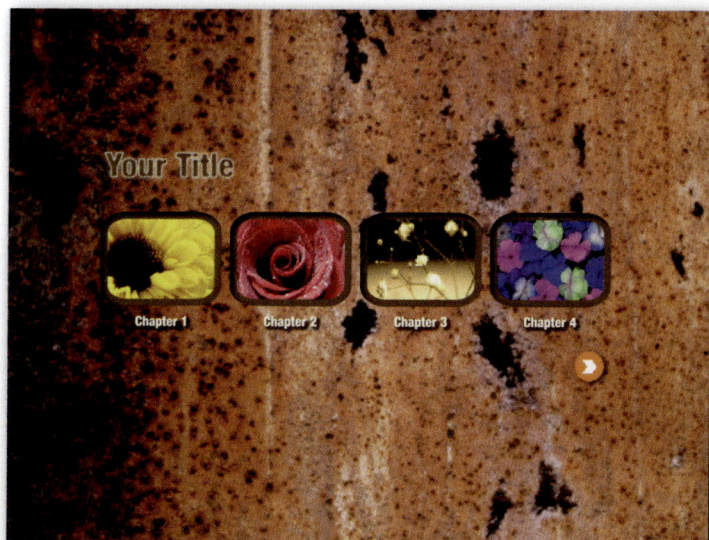

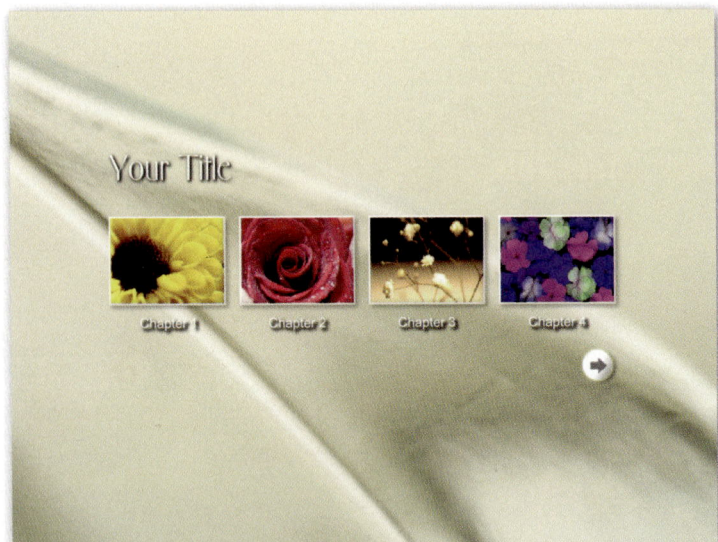

Your Title

Chapter 1 Chapter 2 Chapter 3 Chapter 4

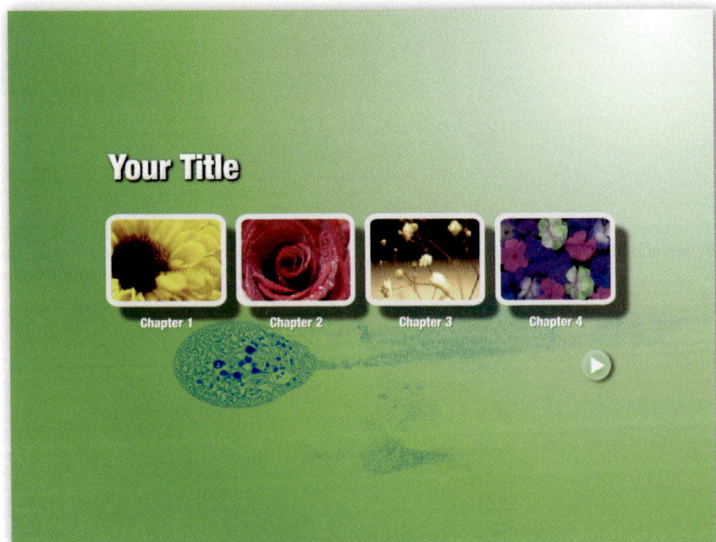

Your Title

Chapter 1 Chapter 2 Chapter 3 Chapter 4

Your Title

Chapter 1

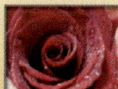
Chapter 2

Chapter 3

Chapter 4

General

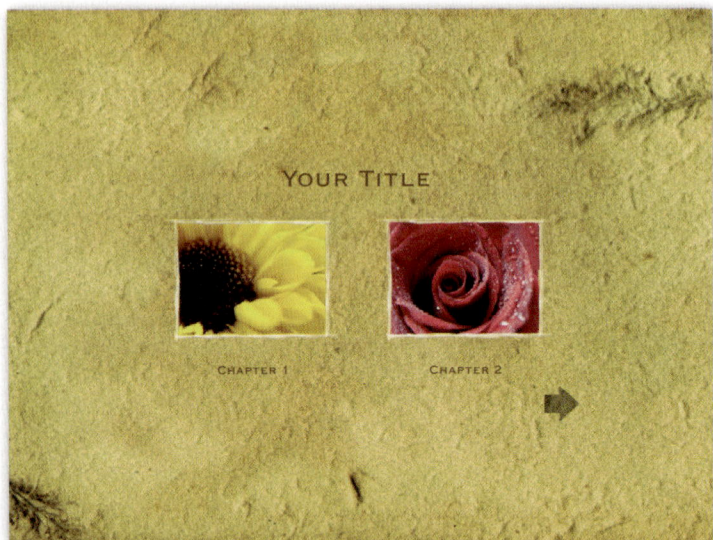

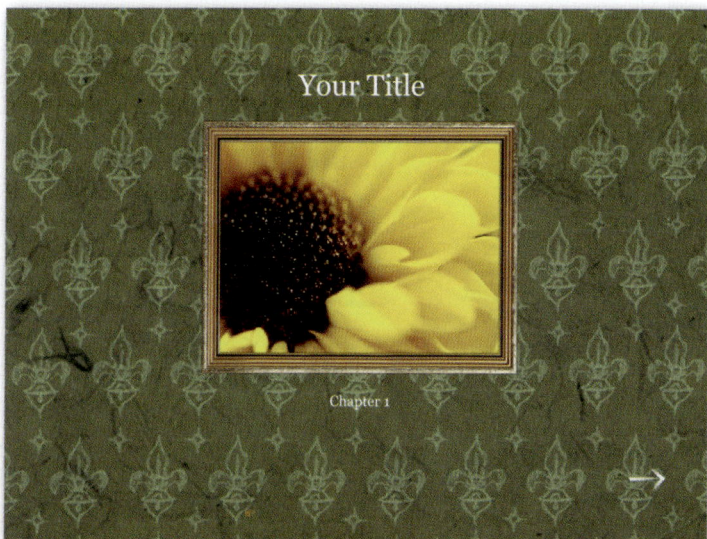

Your Title

Chapter 1

Your Title

Chapter 1   Chapter 2   Chapter 3

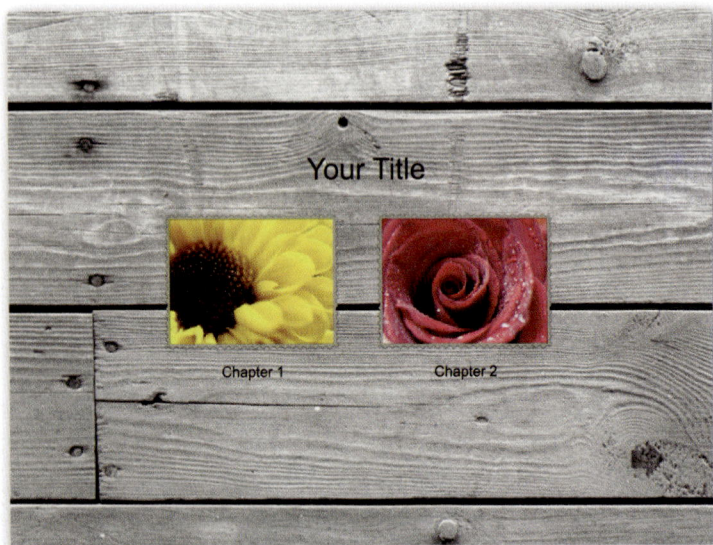

Your Title

Chapter 1   Chapter 2

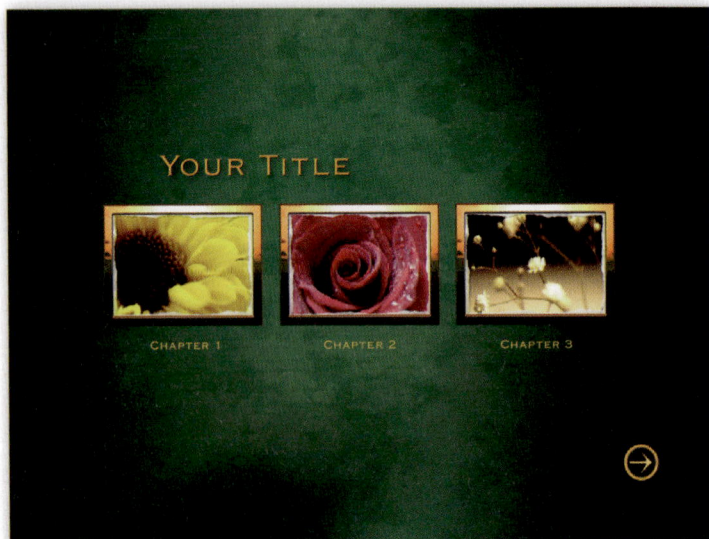

YOUR TITLE

CHAPTER 1   CHAPTER 2   CHAPTER 3

Your Title

Chapter 1

Chapter 2

CHAPTER 1

CHAPTER 2

CHAPTER 3

YOUR TITLE

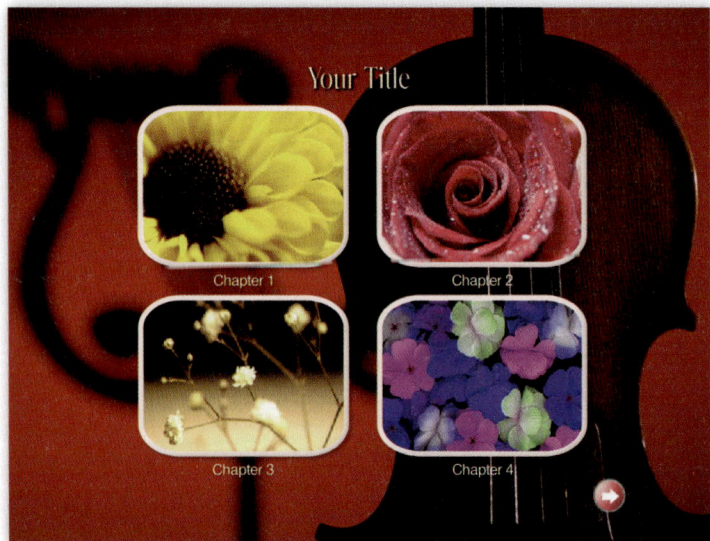

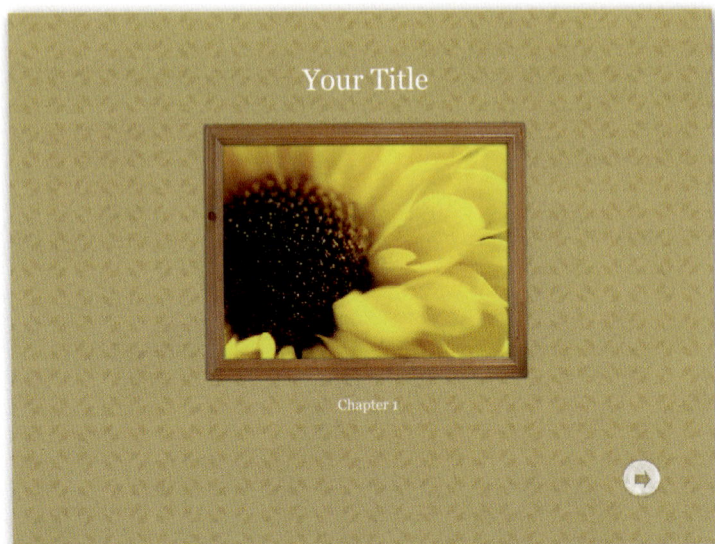

Your Title

Chapter 1

Your Title

Chapter 1   Chapter 2   Chapter 3

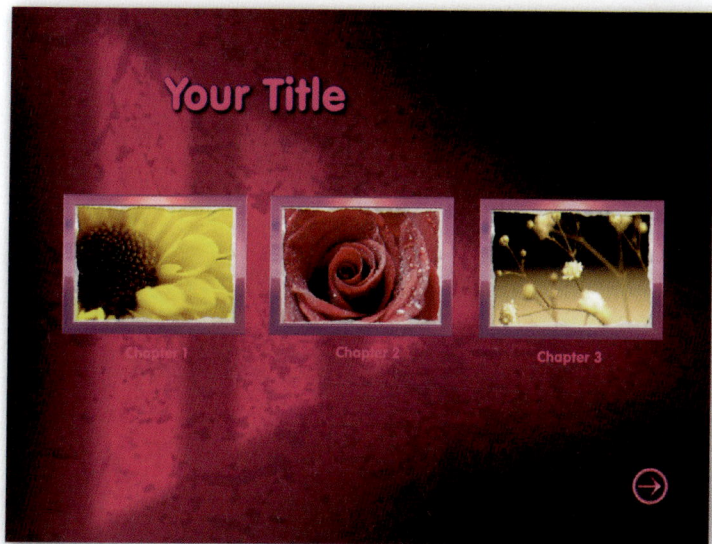

Holidays and Festivities

Home

Kids and Baby

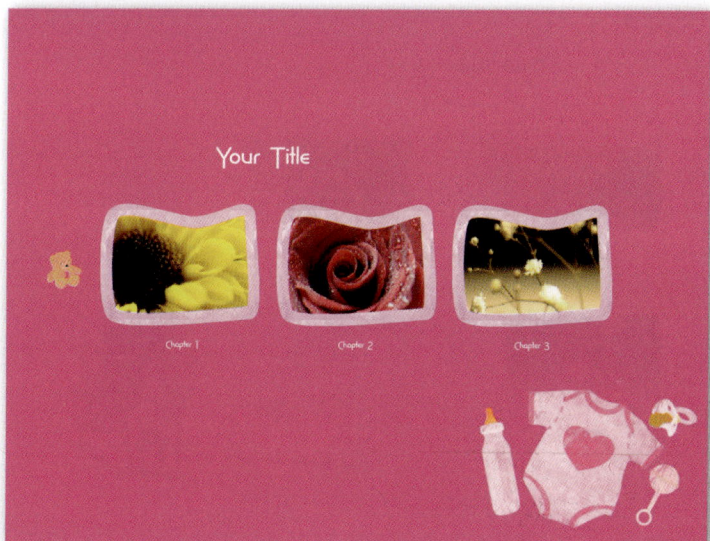

Your Title

Chapter 1

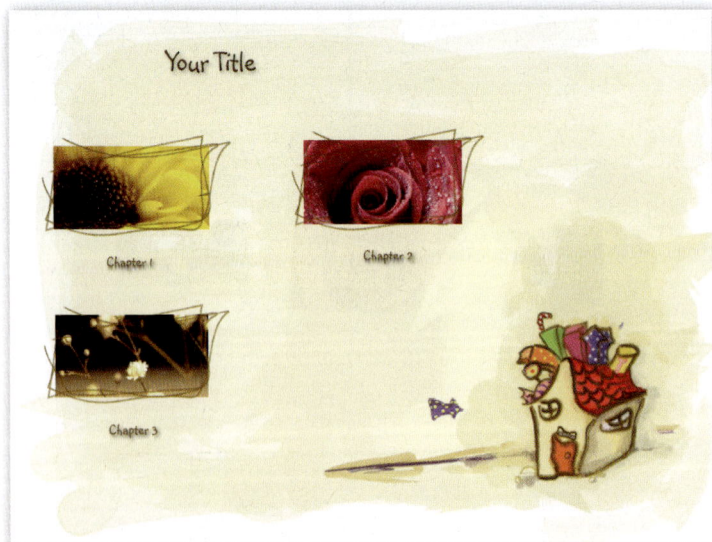

Your Title

Chapter 1

Chapter 2

Chapter 3

Chapter 1

Your Title

YOUR TITLE

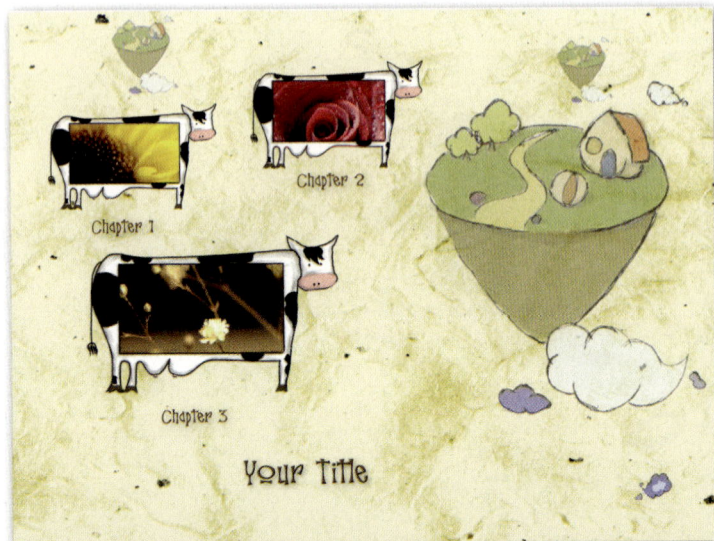

Chapter 1

Chapter 2

Chapter 3

Your Title

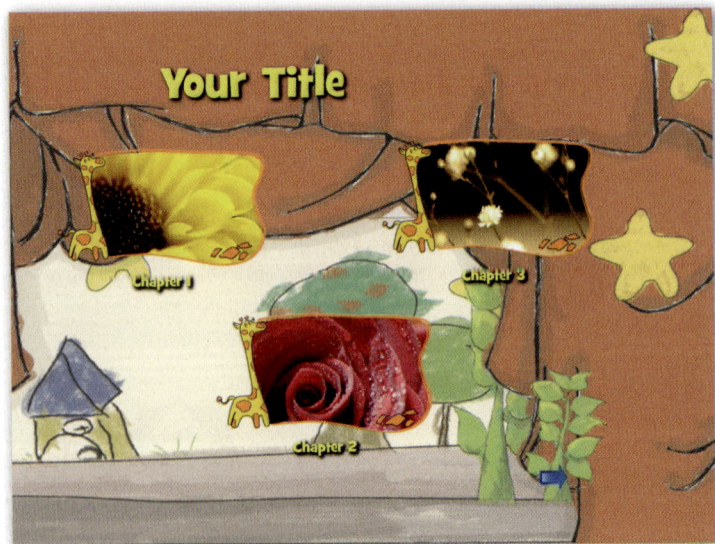

Your Title

Chapter 1

Chapter 2

Chapter 3

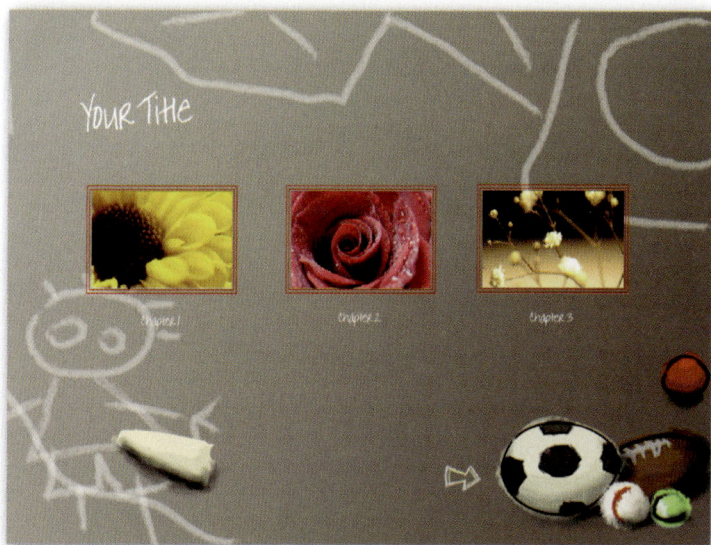

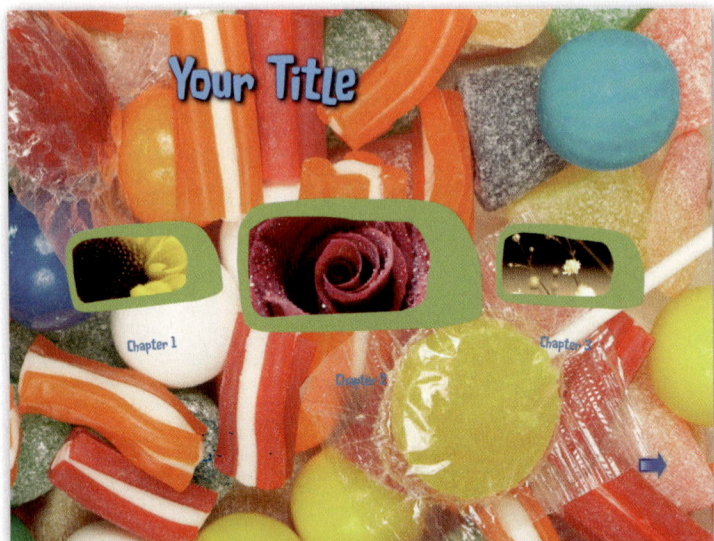

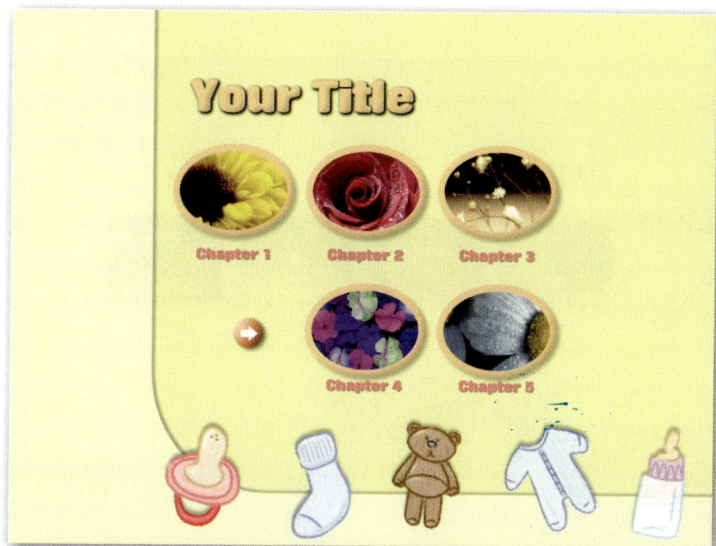

Your Title

Chapter 1   Chapter 2   Chapter 3   Chapter 4

Modern

Your Title

Chapter 1   Chapter 2   Chapter 3   Chapter 4

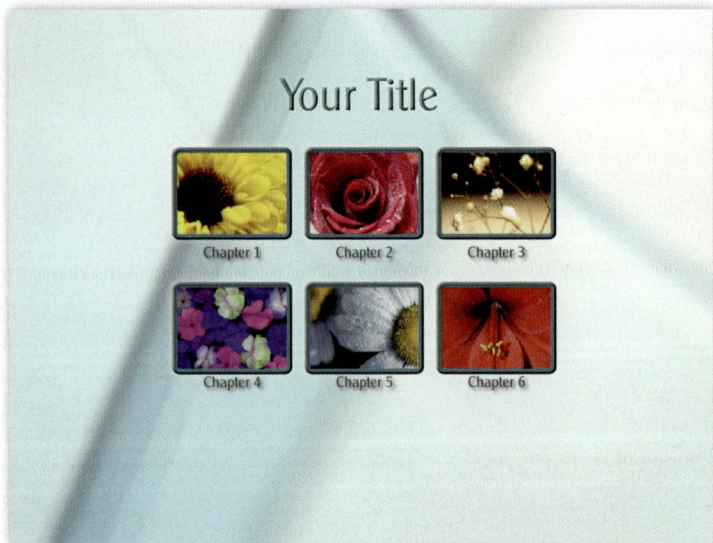

Your Title

Chapter 1   Chapter 2   Chapter 3

Chapter 4   Chapter 5   Chapter 6

Moods

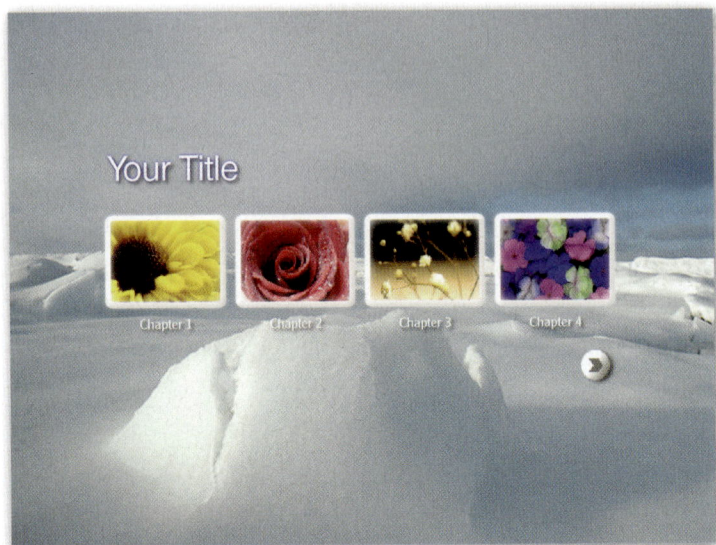

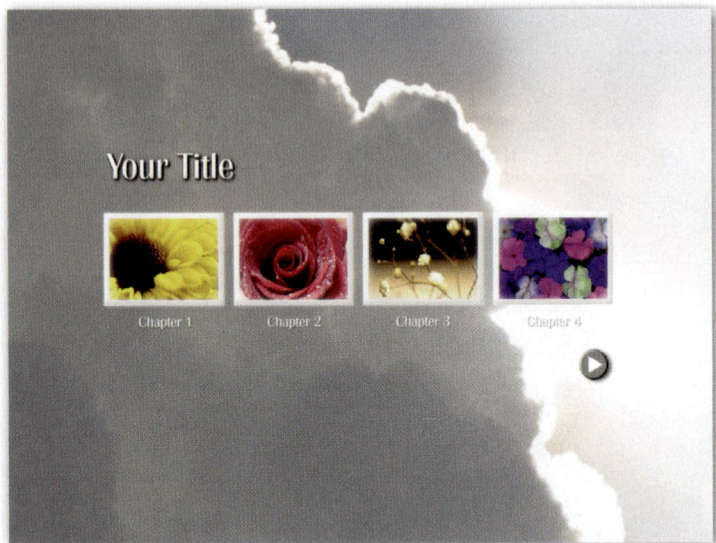

Your Title

Chapter 1   Chapter 2   Chapter 3   Chapter 4

Movie Styles

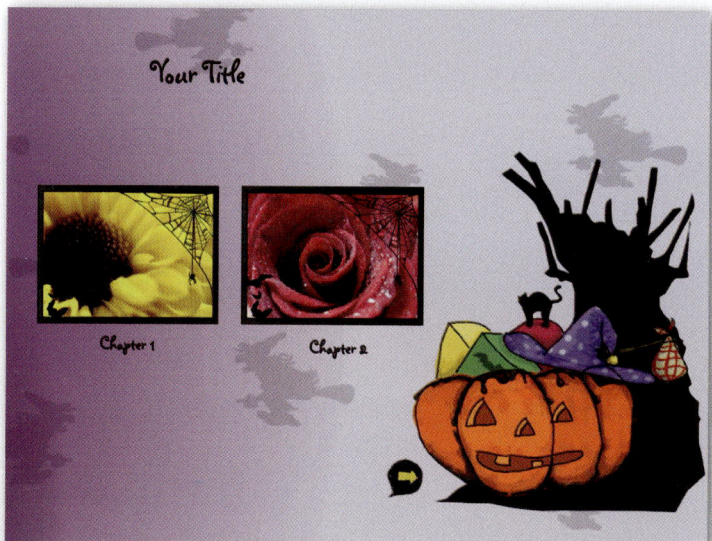

Seasons

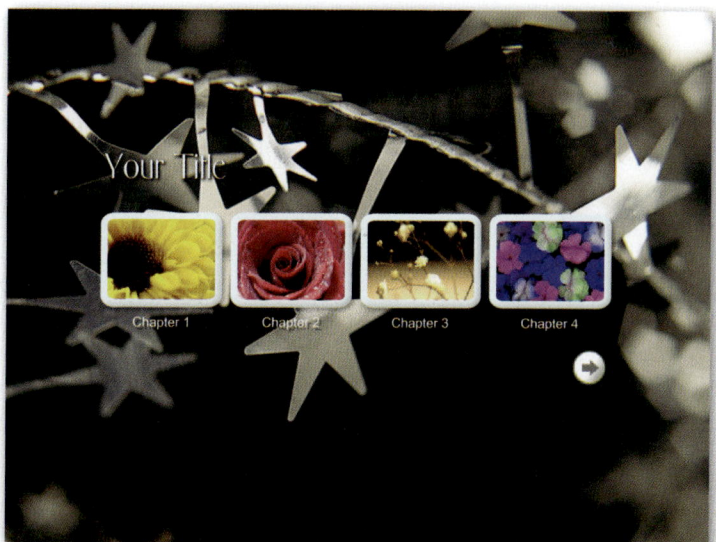

Sports

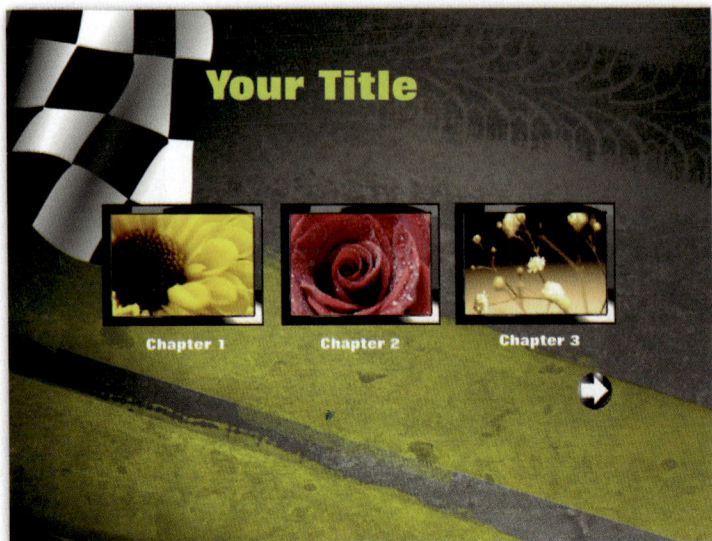

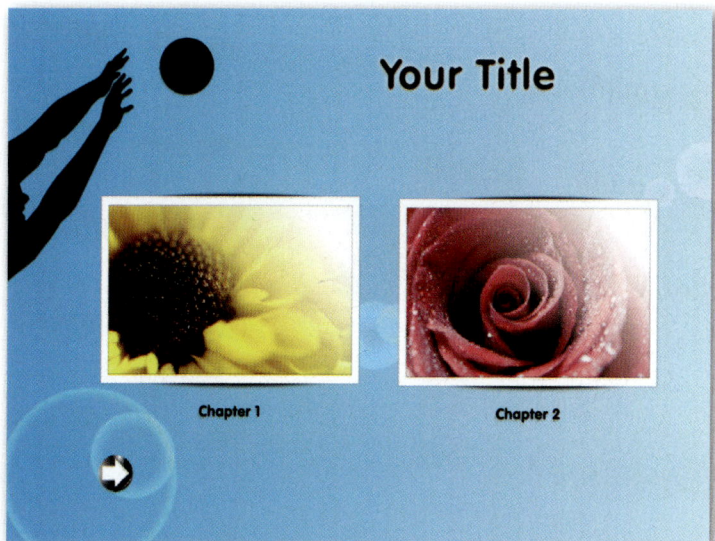

Wedding and Romance

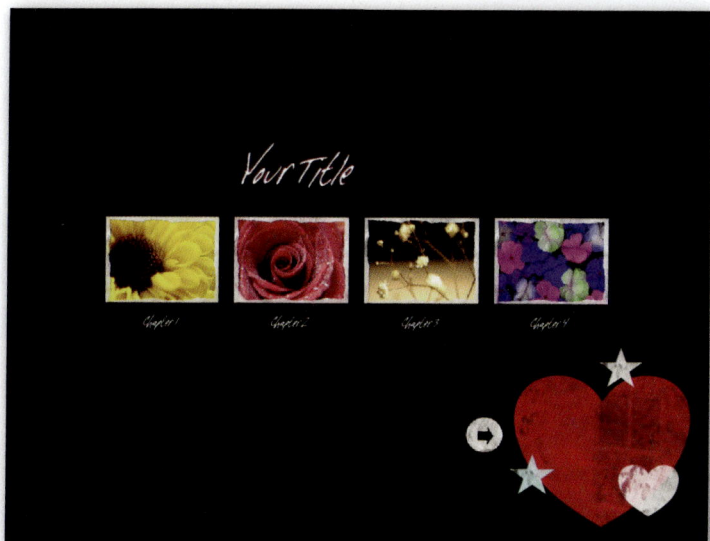

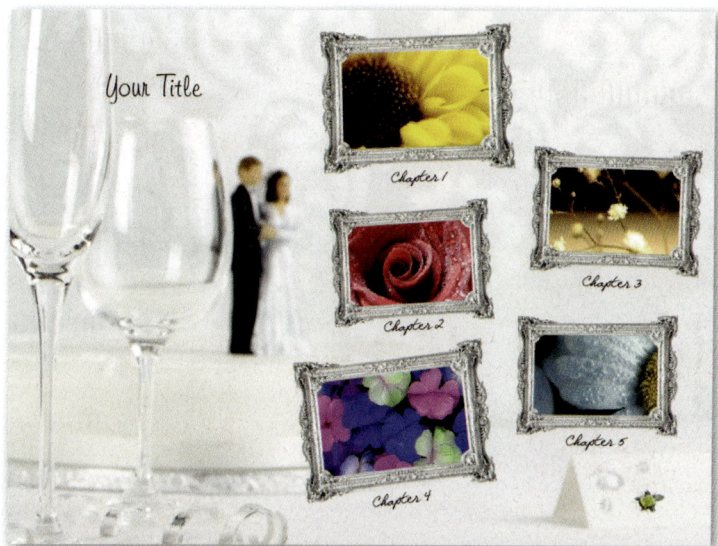

Your Title

Chapter 1

Chapter 2

Chapter 3

Chapter 4

Chapter 5

Your Title

Chapter 1

Chapter 2

Chapter 3

Chapter 4

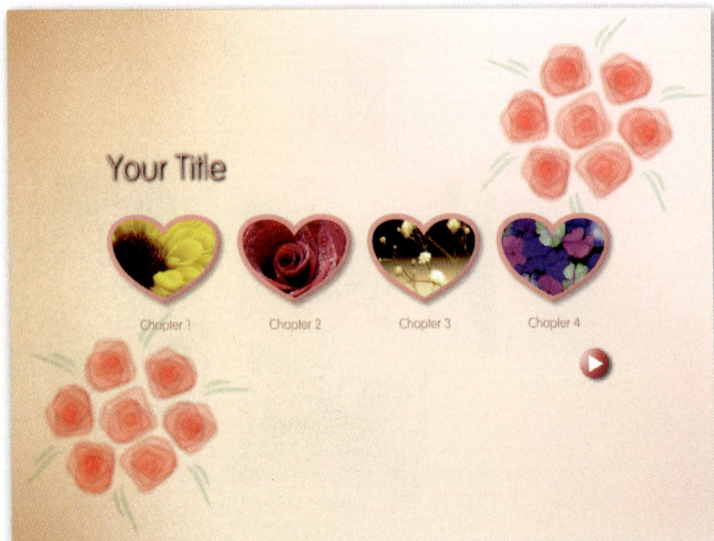

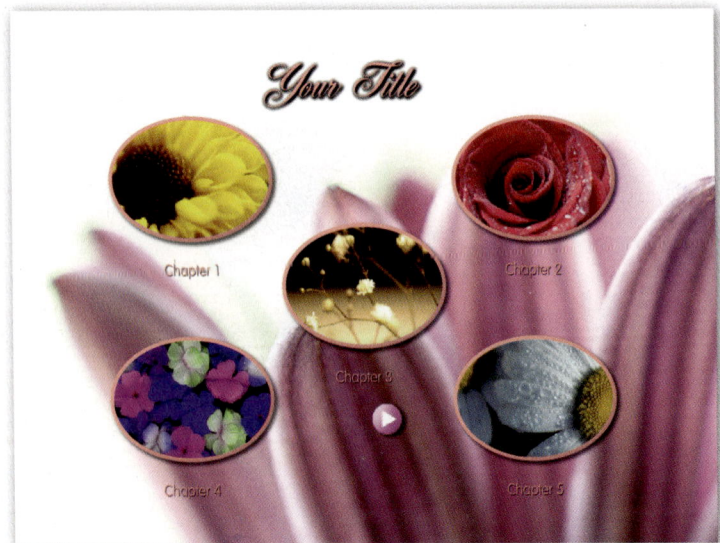